# When Roots Die

*Patricia Jones-Jackson*

# When Roots Die

## Endangered Traditions on the Sea Islands

The University of Georgia Press
Athens and London

© 1987 by the University of Georgia Press
Athens, Georgia 30602
All rights reserved
Designed by Dariel Mayer
Set in Mergenthaler Linotron 202 Times Roman
with display in Cheltenham Book
The paper in this book meets the guidelines for
permanence and durability of the Committee on
Production Guidelines for Book Longevity of the
Council on Library Resources.

Printed in the United States of America
91  90  89  88  87    5  4  3  2  1

Library of Congress Cataloging in Publication Data

Jones-Jackson, Patricia.
  When roots die.

  Bibliography: p.
  Includes index.
  1. Sea Islands — Social life and customs.   2.
Gullah dialect.   3. Afro-Americans — Sea Islands
— Social life and customs.   I. Title.
F277.B3J675   1987     306'.09757'99
85-20912
ISBN 0-8203-0833-1 (alk. paper)

For Miss Myma
and the people of the Sea Islands

# Contents

# Foreword

The Sea Islands are low and flat, and they have a beauty beyond description. When I was a child growing up in the South Carolina lowcountry, we used to take Sunday afternoon drives. If we went down from Charleston across the Ashley River and Wappoo Creek onto James Island and then across the Stono River onto Johns Island, we saw great live oaks leaning dreamily over the road. I remember (or perhaps I imagine) that their low branches, almost hidden by gloomy, gray moss, seemed to enclose the road into long miles of gray tunnel. Here and there we passed through swampy lowlands. I was told that in such places snakes and alligators (and haunts and plat-eyes) were lying in wait for bad little boys and girls. The tangled vines and underbrush had a menacing and sinister beauty. Here and there, too, the oak-lined avenue was broken by fields and pastures. Mules and cows dozed and switched flies under a torrid sun. Rainfall seemed an ancient memory: there were spots where the grass sometimes seemed to have abandoned the effort to be green. And here and there families of black people waved from the porches of small, gray, weather-stained cabins. Shouting children and barking dogs chased one another across neatly swept yards. I can still recall the fresh clouds of fragrance wafted in from the nearby salt marsh and the soft sound of pine needles rustling in the breeze.

Atlantic waves break upon a series of barrier islands all along the coast of Georgia and South Carolina. Tidal streams and inlets, draining an intricate system of shallow, marsh-filled coastal lagoons, separate them from the mainland and from one another. From Waties Island in the mouth of Little River near the North and South Carolina line south past the wide beaches and thick dunes of the Grand Strand; past Pawleys and North islands to Georgetown; from South, Cedar, and Murphy islands to Cape Romaine; down past Bull, Capers, and Dewees islands and the Isle of Palms to Charleston; from James and Johns, past Kiawah, Wadmalaw, and Edisto islands to Beaufort; down past St. Helena, Hunting, Fripp, and Parris islands; past Hilton Head and Daufuski to Savannah; from Tybee, Wassaw, Ossabaw, and St. Catherines to Sapelo; past St. Simons and Jekyll islands to Cumberland on the Georgia-Florida border—the Sea Islands guard the coast. The coastline is intersected not only by Winyah and Bull bays, Charleston Harbor, and St. Helena, Port Royal, Sapelo, and St. Andrew sounds, but also by many lesser inlets curling around the Sea Islands. Bounded on one side by the ocean and on the other by the salt marsh, these Sea Islands use the energy of wind and wave to build sand barriers that protect the mainland from storm and surf.

The Sea Islands north of Charleston are often older beach resorts such as Pawleys Island and the Isle of Palms. Their residents and visitors are mainly white. Other islands are wildlife sanctuaries such as the 31,000-acre Cape Romaine National Wildlife Refuge, the 20,000-acre Tom Yawkee Wildlife Center on South Island, and the 17,000-acre Belle W. Baruch research facilities on Hobcaw Barony. They serve as home for such endangered species as the bald eagle, the Eastern brown pelican, the short-nosed sturgeon, and the loggerhead turtle. Many islands south of Charleston are populated entirely or primarily by blacks, whose venerable folk culture and vivid creole language are the subject of this book. On the coastal mainland adjacent to the Sea Islands are black people who share that folk culture and that creole language. While they are not—strictly speaking—Sea Islanders, in many ways this book tells their story too.

For two centuries this coastal region has been the home of enslaved Africans and their descendants. Theirs is a sad but inspiring story. They built—in a very literal sense—the plantations, and they tilled the rich fields of rice, indigo, or Sea Island cotton. Some of the slaves were brought to the Sea Islands by Barbadian planters who migrated to the Carolina colony in the seventeenth and eighteenth centuries as a refuge from the overcrowding of Barbados. Many more were imported directly from Africa. By the American Revolution the slaves, from various parts of Africa and from various ethnic and linguistic groups, had already created a distinctive culture. During the Civil War, when white planter families fled the Sea Islands before the invading Union troops, Sea Island blacks began to cultivate the land for themselves. Hundreds of them joined the Union Army in the celebrated First South Carolina Volunteers. On January 16, 1865, General William Tecumseh

Sherman's famous Special Field Order No. 15 set aside for the former slaves "the islands from Charleston south [and] the abandoned rice fields along the rivers for thirty miles back from the sea." Within weeks black homesteaders were happily farming their own plots on Edisto, Wadmalaw, Johns, and James islands. By September, President Andrew Johnson had nullified Sherman's order. Many freedmen were dispossessed, but others tenaciously held on to their lands and passed them on to their descendants. Some even managed to buy more land at the end of the nineteenth century as whites again abandoned the islands after years of feeble cotton prices and a series of killer hurricanes. For the first half of the twentieth century blacks continued to be in the majority on the Sea Islands, and land values continued to be low.

For generations the Sea Islanders lived under the same hot sun, surrounded by the same sea and salt marsh, forming a barrier that isolated them from the mainland. For generations fishermen flung their nets into creeks and marshes and ocean for crabs, shrimp, and fish; and they gathered oysters and clams. These supplied both local markets and their own kitchens. For generations islanders cultivated their own little plots of land. Farmers hoed the loamy soil of the islands to produce crops of beans, peas, and cotton. First there was the planting, then the weeding, then the reaping. In the winter women sewed clothes and made quilts; the men looked for work ashore. In the spring they started the cycle over from the beginning—the planting, the weeding, the reaping.

The years passed: the young grew old and the old died. And the planting, seeding, and reaping, and the fishing, shrimping, and crabbing went on. And each spring the cycle started over again. Each year was like the year before. Each generation was like the generation before. For generations there were the same prayers and the same hopes, the same faith and the same fear, the same work and the same result. For generations there was the same old, hard legacy of slavery that robbed men and women of their honor, a legacy visited upon the children and the grandchildren and the great-grandchildren, a legacy against which honest hard work seemed useless, a legacy so old it took its place among natural phenomena like the wind and the rain.

It was not an easy life; but it was a self-sufficient life adapted to the environment, a life shaped by a rich folk culture. Cut off from the mainland, generations of Sea Islanders preserved their cultural heritage, reflecting both continuity with Africa and creativity in the New World.

Perhaps most important, Gullah—the creole language developed by the slaves on the Sea Islands and in the South Carolina and Georgia low-country—continued to be the language in which their folk culture was passed down to posterity. Proverbs, metaphors of social experience, continued to reflect the African preference for speaking by indirection; and African naming patterns persisted on the Sea Islands. For generations, folktales of the audacious animal trickster Ber Rabbit and of the no less audacious slave trickster John blended elements of African folk narrative with elements of the Sea Islanders' historical experience. For generations talented Sea Island artisans created traditional arts and crafts such as coiled sweetgrass baskets and strip quilts. Out of this tradition one Sea Islander, Philip Simmons of Daniel Island, became Charleston's preeminent artist in wrought-iron gates. For generations folk medicine of both the pharmaceutical and the psychological varieties continued to heal the sick on the Sea Islands, and natural phenomena continued to serve as signs foretelling the future, whether changing weather or impending death. Ghosts or haunts—the spirits of the dead—returned from time to time to trouble the living, although local conjurers (assisted by various substances held to be magical) helped to ward off their unwelcome visits. For generations Sea Islanders entertained their children with play songs after the day's work was done. At night they sang the children to sleep with lullabies. On Saturday nights they held dances and frolics. Their folk version of Christianity retained the earliest "shouting" styles of singing spirituals, in which the African religious phenomenon of spirit possession remained vividly linked with prayer, music, and bodily movement. No one thought this way of life would change. The life of the land and the people seemed fixed in an invisible circle, enclosed by the waters and the passage of time.

And then something happened. It did not seem revolutionary at the time. In 1950 Georgia timber magnate General Joseph B. Fraser and his associates bought large tracts of land on the southern end of Hilton Head Island. At first they simply cut down the ancient stands of timber. But soon his son Charles, a young Yale law school graduate, launched the development of a series of lavish resort "plantations"—Sea Pines, Hilton Head, and Honey Horn—pioneering the "resort island" concept. In 1956 the first bridge to Hilton Head Island was constructed. Feverish land speculation ensued as other developers scurried onto Hilton Head and other Sea Islands to exploit the boom, buying up land from black islanders and building more resorts.

Hilton Head Island became known as a resort for the affluent. But similar developments have taken place on other Sea Islands. Hilton Head appears in many ways to have forecast what the future would bring. Its recent course is worth closer examination. In 1950 nearly all of the residents of Hilton Head were black; by 1980 they were outnumbered five to one by whites. According to Fraser, development has been a good thing for black natives of the islands. Resort development "caused black-owned land on Hilton Head Island to increase in value from $100 an acre near the beach or near the marshes to $50,000 or $100,000 an acre today. This flows into the pocket of the blacks who elect to sell," he says.

> I sold lots at $7,000 which today sell for $350,000. Some blacks have done the same. Some of them, smarter than I was, held onto their land, as I and developers developed our land and pushed up the values. Now they are selling. I am jubilant, positively jubilant, when a black farm family that has held the land for five generations on Hilton Head Island, land that was worth $100 when we arrived here, sells it today for $50,000. I think that's wonderful.

Fraser contends that

> it is a wise thing, for those who need the money, to elect to sell. Every black family that sells a portion of their heritage that was maintained with great struggle and great effort by their parents and grandparents and great-grandparents, and uses a part of that heritage to send a child to engineering school or to boarding school, is making an investment in the future of that family. I wish more of them would do it.

The emergence of Hilton Head Island as a playground for rich white northerners, in the opinion of Charles Fraser, has been beneficial for everyone.

But others are less sanguine. "We have witnessed some changes on Hilton Head over the last twenty-five years," suggests Emory Campbell, a native of the island, "and they have not all been good from the black perspective." Some contend that black landowners were induced to sell their land too cheaply—either through trickery or because they did not know the land's fair market value. Unquestionably some black families made money on the transactions, at least by comparison with the barterlike economy of the predevelopment decades. But even those who received fair prices made money at the cost of selling their birthright. For those who were unwilling to sell, rising land values only meant rising property taxes. Many were forced to sell because they could no longer afford to keep up the additional tax burden. "We have witnessed land being sold because the family no longer wanted to tolerate taxes on land that's doing nothing," Campbell stresses. A money economy has come to Hilton Head and the other Sea Islands. Land is being sold, he points out, "merely because people, families, need the money."*

The resort island rich give Beaufort County, which includes Hilton Head and other Sea Islands, the second highest per capita income in South Carolina. But unemployment in the county surpasses the state average with depressing regularity. And half the county's nonagricultural employees work in low-paying service jobs—as caddies, cooks, maids, maintenance workers, waiters, and waitresses. It is certainly true that this generation of islanders is better paid than the generation before them; it is not necessarily true that they are economically better off. But the islanders now live in a money economy. They must earn money to live.

While low-paying service jobs are easily available on the resort islands, higher-paying skilled occupations are rare. And those positions are not normally filled by islanders, who usually lack the requisite education. Incentives to acquire an education for positions that seem to be set aside for outsiders are lacking; incentives to take the low-paying jobs are abundant. The situation "enslaves" young people, says Emory Campbell. "They forget that a job is only a means to an end." Sea Island blacks "are not motivated to go beyond the tenth, eleventh grade because they see the immediacy of the dollar," he notes. But education does not seem to break the cycle on the Sea Islands. "The few that have gone to college, they're motivated to leave rather than to stay. They can't tolerate the situation. We just don't have the kinds of jobs here that would dignify staying. They become overwhelmed by the subservient roles that most blacks are put in here."

*I was present at the exchange between Charles E. Fraser and Emory Campbell in Charleston on December 3, 1982. The occasion was a conference entitled "Coastal Development: Past, Present, and Future," organized by the Coastal Heritage Program of the South Carolina Sea Grant Consortium with support from the South Carolina Committee for the Humanities. Their remarks are printed in the proceedings of the conference, pp. 55–56, 63. Additional comments by Campbell are taken from "We Are an Endangered Species: An Interview with Emory Campbell," by Vernie Singleton, *Southern Exposure* 10 (May–June, 1982): 37–39.

Fraser is sensitive to charges that hiring practices are discriminatory. "I get continued crap that we should confine our employment exclusively to people who were born on Hilton Head Island, without regard to their ability or what they do," he complains. "When we had a vice president for personnel, black, college educated, graduate degree in personnel management, we got nothing but hell because he had not been born on Hilton Head Island. This is the sort of crap we get over and over again." Fraser's preference for well-qualified employees to fill upper-echelon positions is understandable. But the fact remains that of all the jobs created by development on the Sea Islands, virtually the only ones which are available to the Sea Islanders themselves are jobs as servants.

Even more striking than the economic consequences of development on the indigenous population of the Sea Islands has been its cultural impact. Modernization has caused severe social dislocations. "Developers just come in and roll over whoever is there," charges Emory Campbell, "move them out or roll over them and change their culture, change their way of life, destroy the environment, and therefore the culture has to be changed." Perhaps the unintentional vanguard of white cultural imperialism has been the school. Campbell calls for a school system "that is in tune with the culture of the black child of this island. That child's heritage," he notes, "is different from a child who came here from Chicago, New York, or Ohio. And that's where a lot of our white kids are coming from; so you put them in a classroom and say you're integrated and you've got a classroom situation at Hilton Head Elementary School that's oriented to those kids who are moving in." Teachers with little understanding of the islands' rich historical and cultural heritage criticize the island children's Gullah speech—as though the children were the outsiders who speak funny! They do not know that Gullah is a creole language with a very regular syntax and phonology of its own. They do not know that other forms of the islanders' cultural expression are parts of an ancient and beautiful tradition with a rich history behind it. It is little wonder that many Sea Island children—in the face of daily assaults on the way they talk and the way they express themselves—see the school as the enemy, taking away more than it gives. With white dominance of the economic and educational systems some Sea Islanders have become ashamed of their culture. Thus the schools, intended to be the agents of cultural enrichment, have become agents of cultural destruction.

There is a story that during the 1930s an aged black man on one of the Sea Islands was asked how he was faring in the Great Depression. "Dat Depression new-come," he replied. "Ah bin-hyuh. *New-come* can't beat *bin-hyuh.*" The Sea Islands survived the Great Depression, but now they suffer from what the historian Eric Hobsbawm calls "the impact of social transformation." The old coexists uneasily with the new, *bin-hyuh* with *come-hyuh;* but *bin-hyuh* is on the defensive. Not even those islands that have thus far eluded the bulldozers have immunity to development. To endure, a community must be able to bequeath its shared traditional expressive culture to the next generation. Without the living context in which that expressive culture arises, cultural endurance is by no means certain. It is not the wildlife of the islands that is the most endangered, says Emory Campbell. "*We* have become the new endangered species."

This book is an act of cultural conservation. Patricia Jones-Jackson knew and loved the people of the Sea Islands and their rich folk culture. Here she vividly presents some of those people and some of that folk culture. In these pages the old talk and the old tales, the old prayers and the old personal expressiveness come vibrantly to life. The talk and tales and prayers and expressions are more than just quaint cultural artifacts. They have provided the islanders with a sense of continuity with generations gone before, a precious lifeline to courageous ancestors who survived slavery and endured generations of poverty. That heritage is a source of strength that has enabled them to cope with the hail and upheaval of life. As we drift further and further out upon the sea of modernization, that heritage may be as crucial to our sanity and survival as to theirs. The Sea Islanders and their folk culture have something precious to offer us if we do not destroy them first.

*When Roots Die* makes an important contribution to the fields of linguistics and folklore. Both folklorists and linguists can learn much from these interdisciplinary explorations. What makes this a really important book, however, is the fact that it is the first book-length treatment of contemporary Gullah language and culture that combines sound scholarship with a clear and engaging style accessible to non-linguists and nonfolklorists. Readers will find that it can be read for pleasure, but not without profit. It reaches beyond scholars to provide a general audience—teachers, school principals, employers, librarians, lawyers, legislators, judges, newcomers and visitors to the islands, and (one hopes) developers themselves—with a stimulating introduction to the language and culture of the Gullah-speaking people of the South Carolina and Georgia Sea Islands. This book can help neighbors to understand one another better. It tells the truth about the people of the Sea Islands and their endangered traditions in a fresh and meaningful way.

—Charles Joyner

# In Memoriam

She was beautiful. That was the first thing most people noticed about Patricia Jones-Jackson. Those who knew her found her inner beauty—her charm and kindness and intelligence—even more striking than her appearance. Hers was a very special grace.

She was born on August 14, 1946, in Arkansas and died on June 29, 1986, from injuries received in an automobile accident the day before on Johns Island, South Carolina. She is survived by her husband, Sidney, and three children: fourteen-year-old Patricia Antonia, eleven-year-old Sidney, and four-year-old Brie Ann. An orphaned nephew, eighteen-year-old Benjie Jackson, is also part of her family.

Her death cut short an academic career of unusual promise. She graduated from the University of Detroit in 1970. She earned her Ph.D. in linguistics at the University of Michigan in 1978 with a dissertation entitled "The Status of Gullah: An Investigation of Convergent Processes." The excellence of her dissertation and of her articles in *Anthropological Linguistics* and *The Journal of Religious Thought* led to her appointment to the faculty of Howard University, where she was a member of the English department at the time of her death.

Patricia Jones-Jackson was a gifted scholar who was equally at home in the library or in the field. In fact, she was engaged in fieldwork—on assignment for the *National Geographic Magazine*—when she died. The ability to write rich, clear English prose is infrequent. The ability to perform truly interdisciplinary analysis is even less common. The ability to do both at the same time is rare. Patricia will be remembered best by the scholarly world not just for her analytical acumen or her writing style but for her great love and respect for the people whose language and culture she studied and wrote about. This book is her legacy to the scholarly world of which she was a part and to those Gullah-speaking people into whose lives she came.

# Preface

The black inhabitants of the Sea Islands, located off the coast of Georgia and South Carolina, have provided researchers with a reservoir of distinctively African and African-American cultural roots. Their unique society has been developed, nurtured, and maintained by the geographical isolation of the islands, the social and economic independence of the islanders, and the marginal contact with residents outside the Sea Island area. These factors have created and fostered an environment within which the inhabitants—West African slaves, ex-slaves, and their free ancestors—have been able to reinforce vigorous traditions characteristic of their culture, and to perpetuate communities with concentrations of African influences paralleled by no other black areas in the United States. Remnants of these African traditions were passed on to the islanders through narrative tales, religious practices, burial ceremonies, language patterns, and other practices, only some of which have been recorded by linguists, sociologists, anthropologists, and folklorists.

Today changes are being brought to the islands, and the Sea Island culture is declining under the resulting social pressures. On the one hand, outsiders, particularly white Americans, Arabs, and other foreigners, are moving to the area and in some instances commercializing entire islands. On the other hand, the building of bridges has brought about easier access to many of the islands and better educational facilities and job opportunities for their inhabitants. As would be expected, such forces are motivating a break in cultural traditions, an upheaval of social patterns, and a general disruption of the old norms, all of which are now in some danger of becoming lost.

This book is structured to provide a comprehensive view of the Sea Island culture and literature and of the Gullah (or, as it is called in Georgia, Geechee) language. Chapter 1 is devoted primarily to a survey of the area and its people. I judge it important to provide a full description of the geography, demography, and economic and social history of the region, because only in an environment like that of the Sea Islands could the inhabitants have maintained the level of continuity with African culture that has been recorded (and that surely remains to be recorded).

Chapters 2 and 3 constitute the greatest portion of the book. Chapter 2 provides detailed descriptions of the settings in which the tales are told and the telling techniques employed, and sketches of some of the most prolific storytellers. Chapter 3 is composed of Gullah prayers and tales, with translations of some African counterparts. This section may be particularly pleasing to those interested in seeing just how closely the Gullah tales compare with African narratives.

Chapter 4 provides a description of those linguistic features in contemporary Gullah speech which have African parallels. This chapter may be especially useful in helping to delineate features characteristic of Gullah and not characteristic of inland African-American speech or of other speech varieties in the United States. In addition to providing insights into the status of present-day Gullah on the Sea Islands, Chapter 4 is germane to the interested reader's understanding of certain linguistic features of the Gullah speech samples.

Most often we get only a retrospective look at a culture after many of its unique features have been lost. One of the great attractions of the Sea Islands for students of the humanities and social sciences is that the expected slow pace of change in remote areas will permit a look into the culture as it undergoes transition. As outside forces erode the traditional social structure of the islanders, every attempt should be made to maintain a record of changing language, attitudes, and oral traditions. And as I hope to show in this book, researchers who come with the right preparation and receptive minds can make their studies as rewarding for the islanders as for the investigators.

In my own case, I decided that given the wide field of untapped resources in the Sea Island area, it would be wise to undertake my investigation in collaboration with a colleague from a field other than linguistics. Behavioral data, whether dealing with folklore, language, cognition, or their interrelationships, have in the past tended to be rigidly segmented and compartmentalized into folklore, linguistics, psychology, sociology, or anthropology. The needs for interdisciplinary approaches to the study of human behavior, however, and for exchanges of information and ideas among scholars in related fields, are becoming increasingly more apparent.[1]

Accordingly, during the first two years of my research on the Sea Islands, I worked with Faith Mitchell, an anthropologist who had spent several years in the area. Faith's assistance in helping me to understand the similarities and differences between Sea Island practices and those of certain peoples of Africa was invaluable. She introduced me to several families in the Wadmalaw community and pointed out such African survivals in the culture as iron casting, fishing techniques, and family practices that she, as an anthropologist, recognized quickly but I, as a linguist, did not.

The interdisciplinary approach also provided reciprocal rewards for her. Since "root medicine" always generated lively conversation, I often used it as a topic for gathering linguistic data. Faith accompanied me on what she called my "collecting trips," became interested in the topic, and later wrote a book on the subject called *Hoodoo Medicine*.

Any attempt to study a culture without adequate knowledge of its language, social structure, and history will be abortive, producing disappointing results. To avoid this danger, I decided to familiarize myself with as much of the literature of the Sea Island area as possible by preparing a bibliography of readings in linguistics, literature, anthropology, folklore, history, and sociology. In assembling a working bibliography, I included such sources as travel guides, local newspapers, magazines, dialect dictionaries, government reports, and miscellaneous publications of local societies. Information from sources of this nature will often, I learned, give detail to geography, climatic conditions, food sources, drug use, towns, cities, ocean and bridge conditions, and the like, in addition to suggesting social contacts.[2]

One usually arrives at a research design or an objective through intense reading and inquiry into one's target area. Without such theoretical preparation, one will have little, if any, idea what problems need solving. It took an immersion in the historical circumstances that have produced the language and culture of the Sea Islands to make me satisfied that I would recognize an Africanism when I heard one. In any research study, of course, defining and analyzing the research design before field exploration begins will both expose facts relevant to solving the problem and determine the methods and approaches which are likely to be most effective for the study. One has to decide where the work will be done, the probable time necessary for effective investigation, the material and data needed to solve the problem, and the field procedures most likely to be useful.[3]

Preparing a research design is one thing; actual entrance into a Sea Island community is quite another. Because the islanders are suspicious of all outsiders, one group of investigators has suggested that research in the islands and in other black communities be conducted in conjunction with local, community-controlled agencies that provide services to the communities.[4] These agencies can be asked to verify the integrity of potential Sea Island investigators and to approve the uses to which they plan to put the results of their research. Not only do organizations of this sort have access to a wide range of information that would be useful to the researcher, but the researcher can reciprocate by making available to the agency any useful information that he or she acquires from outside sources. Coordinate research reduces the risk of community exploitation and is likely to produce positive results from the community.

No matter how careful one's planning has been, as I learned quickly, one may find it necessary to deviate from customary methods of assembling data and to adjust the procedures and time allotted for a study to correspond to the temperament and discretion of the informants. For example, included in the preliminaries made in preparation for my research was a word list containing minimal pairs for the elicitation of vowels and consonants. Because the list was long, and the elicitation so painfully slow and exacting, I did not attempt to procure this information until almost two years after my initial investigation. By then the informants knew me well and were willing to tolerate such a tedious procedure. Even with their willing assistance, it took as long as a week, sometimes more, to complete the word list for one informant.

No research design or methodology, of course, can assure a successful investigation in any discipline in the Sea Island communities. In many ways the success or failure of a study becomes dependent on the islanders' response to the personality of the researcher, and their willingness to accept both researcher and project. Of primary importance, one must have a convincing reason for being on a given island. Patricia Nichols, to take one example, acquired entry into a river island community as a teacher—a profession highly valued by the Sea Islanders. According to her, working in a highly visible capacity at a job that made sense for the particular community chosen allowed her to observe and participate in a great variety of speech events.[5]

People in general are often insecure about their particular varieties of speech, and collecting spontaneous speech data can be a problem for anyone conducting a linguistic survey. It is even more of a problem on the Sea Islands because the native speakers of Gullah can and do adjust their speech to produce the closest possible approximations of standard English when they are addressing strangers. To eliminate pressure on the speakers to avoid the creole speech (and to help validate my presence), I explained that one of my objectives for being on the islands was to learn as much as possible about folk medicine "roots," folktales, "lies," and "the old-time talk." I explained, for example, that my grandmother had taught me to identify and collect herbs or roots which were helpful in alleviating certain ailments or even in effecting certain cures. These topics generated much interest and humor; consequently, I was able to assemble a wide store of knowledge concerning medicinal cures, complete with folktales, as well as to collect several varieties of speech data.

Something I learned by sitting through one market day in Charleston illustrates a final point. As I observed an islander selling tomatoes, I realized that she felt much more satisfaction when she sold her goods to a person with whom she had haggled assiduously over the price than when she sold the same amount for a higher price to a well-intentioned but clearly patronizing customer. She had been robbed of the satisfaction of arriving at an "agreed" price. Feelings about the inequality of human beings had been transmitted along with the unequal prices of the tomatoes.

Achieving and maintaining equality in relationships is crucial when striving to establish rapport with informants. Kenneth Goldstein cites a statement to this effect made by Alan Lomax in 1950 during a symposium on data collecting at the Mid-century International Folklore Conference held at Indiana University:

> People say to me that they would like to help me along with my work, that I look as if I need help. And I tell them that I am taking up their time and that I would like to make it up to them. There was never any question of dignity being involved; none of us in our situation was more dignified than anyone else. If the informant liked to drink, I drank, and if he liked to acquire a salary, I haggled with him very hard and very seriously, but we fought over it as equals.[6]

# Acknowledgments

A major portion of this book would consist of names if all the people who contributed in some way were included. Before all others, however, I gratefully acknowledge the people of the Sea Islands, because without their willing cooperation there would have been no book. I am especially indebted to two residents of Wadmalaw Island, Aneatha Brisbane (Miss Myma) and Ida Morris-Hamilton (Miss Ida Mae) for accepting me into their homes and providing me with ties to well-respected island names. Since the islanders know and understand well the meaning of sharing as an inherent part of the extended family, I express my gratitude to the following families rather than to individuals: the Browns, the Williamses, the Pickneys, the Linens, the Jenkinses, the Middletons, the McClouds, the McClures, the Buggs, the Mitchells, the Seabrooks, the Orees, the Smalls, the McDermotts, the Pyatts, the Washingtons, the Mickells, the Gibbses, the Riverses, the Macks, the Ropers, the Higginses, the Simmonses, the Dents, the Fraziers, the Murrays, the Quimbys, the Cummingses, and the Campbells.

I wish to thank the Nigerian people from the Igbo, Yoruba, and Ibebio cultures for their tolerance and patience in helping me to learn their languages and folklore traditions. I offer special thanks to the Ihejetoh family, the Udondek family, the Onunkwo family, and the Konyeers family.

Several friends, colleagues, and professors at the University of Michigan offered assistance and provided guidance for this book in its embryonic stages. These include Rosie Morant Douglas, who first told me about the Sea Island people while sitting in the undergraduate library one afternoon in 1972, and Faith Mitchell, who accompanied me on my first trip to the island communities. I wish also to thank Richard Bailey, J. C. Catford, Peter Fodale, Lemuel Johnson, Patrick Bynoe,

Louise Rounds Ball, and Kathy Eiseley, who gave me the stimulation and encouragement that I needed to begin the project in 1973.

I have also benefited from the knowledge and insights of several linguists, anthropologists, historians, folklorists, and friends from other universities. Outstanding among these is my mentor and friend Professor Charles Joyner, a native of the coastal area and the author of *Down by the Riverside*. He believed, even when I felt that I no longer believed, that the manuscript would become a book. I also acknowledge others who were kind enough to listen or read drafts of the manuscript, honest enough to provide principled criticism, and most of all committed enough to write out lengthy suggestions on how to improve it. I offer special thanks to Ralph Fasold, Fred Cassidy, Dell Hymes, Orlando Taylor, Ian Hancock, Irma Cunningham, Salikoko Mufwene, Michael Montgomery, Lettie Molter, John Rickford, William Stewart, and Molefe Asante.

I warmly acknowledge my long-time friend from the Sea Island area, Dr. G. Franklin Edwards of Howard University, who in the words of the islanders often had to "brace my back against the wall of Zion, and plant my feet deep down in the soil" in order that I might finish this book. Other friends and colleagues who provided willing but "tired" ears include Claudia Tate, Edward Hawthorne, Arnold Wallace, Charles Sessoms, Michael Miller, Lettie Austin, Marshall Banks, Vernon Jones, Karen Michell, Carolyn Stroman, and my typist, Sally McCoy.

I wish to extend special thanks also to Malcolm Call, Ellen Harris, Dariel Mayer, Sandy Hudson, and Douglas Armato at the University of Georgia Press. I am particularly indebted to Janis Bolster, not only because she is a painstakingly proficient editor but because she was "gifted" with the ability to make the most obscure concepts flow easily into prose.

The research for this book was supported by several sources; without their assistance, I would never have been able to complete this study. At the University of Michigan I received a Horace H. Rackham Research Award and a summer grant from the Center for African and Afro-American Studies. At Howard University my work received support from the Faculty Research Program in the Social Sciences, the Humanities and Education Program of the Office of the Vice President for Academic Affairs; and the Graduate School of Arts and Sciences Faculty Grants Program. I was also awarded a WHMM Television Development Grant and a service grant from South Carolina Educational Television. I am especially grateful to Mary Jaffee for her assistance and to the National Endowment for the Humanities for providing funds for this project for a one-year period.

Finally, I wish to acknowledge the generous support of my family: my mother and father, Haller and Curtis Jones, who kept my children while I went to Africa; Grandma Joella and my sisters and brothers, Beryl, Katie, Joycelyn, Phillip, Chester, Charles, and Bernard, who all took turns taking care of my children when I went to the Sea Islands. Most of all, I am grateful to my husband Sidney and our children, Beanie, Antoneia, Brie, and Benji, for tolerating me as I undertook my research. Now Beanie no longer has to ask, "Mommy, haven't you finished yet?"

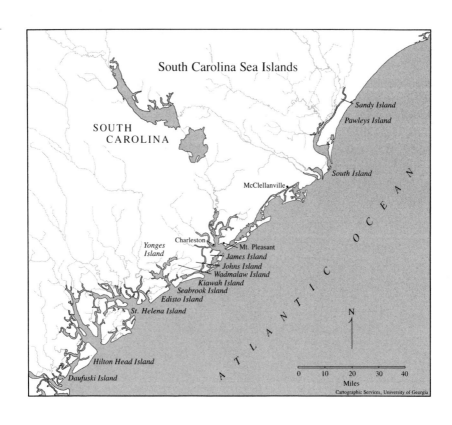

South Carolina Sea Islands

SOUTH
CAROLINA

Sandy Island
Pawleys Island

South Island

McClellanville

Yonges
Island
Charleston
Mt. Pleasant
James Island
Johns Island
Wadmalaw Island
Kiawah Island
Seabrook Island
Edisto Island
St. Helena Island

Hilton Head Island
Daufuski Island

ATLANTIC OCEAN

N

0    10    20    30    40
Miles
Cartographic Services, University of Georgia

# When Roots Die

# Introduction

[i bɪnə dɹɪŋk di βɔɾə
ɛn i gɔt ɹait ɖə ste iə]

*She has partaken of the water,
and she has the right to live here.*

The life-styles, tales, and language peculiarities captured in this book were unearthed during more than nine years of research with the Gullah- or Geechee-speaking Sea Islanders of Georgia and South Carolina and three months of field work in Nigeria, West Africa. Like most Americans, I was in total ignorance of the existence of the Sea Islands for many years—in my case, until 1972. Once I heard about them, no amount of library research and no amount of reading about the Sea Islanders could quench my desire actually to see for myself how they had managed to retain so many more remnants of their West African ancestry than African-Americans in other parts of the country.

On my first trip to the Sea Islands, in 1973, I remember crossing a bridge leading from Charleston to James Island, crossing another one from James Island to Johns Island, and then another one from Johns Island to Wadmalaw. On Wadmalaw the scenery changed drastically, and the farther I drove along the narrow, winding road into the depths of this remote island, the more unusual my surroundings became: hanging moss; dense woodlands; flat, "boggy" swamps; and the musty, sweet aroma of ocean air. A person could get lost forever on these islands, I remember thinking. As I would later learn, it was this very remoteness which contributed to the continuation of the African-derived culture of the Sea Island area.

I turned around a deep bend in the road and continued on, ultimately arriving at New Jerusalem African Methodist Episcopal Church. I attended church service because one must go to church to see the greatest gathering of people, and one must have the minister's sanction for one's work if one is to gain cooperation during the research. I was introduced to the congregation, and after the service the islanders were warm and hospitable, as is the custom on the church ground and as is common practice in many southern communities. But once we left the grounds, most members of the community became very conservative and even hostile concerning the mechanics of their culture. Their reactions to me followed a specific pattern. First they asked, Whose daughter are you? Because I was not the daughter of anyone on the island, the next question was, Who are your people here? As I had no relatives on that island or any island, the next question was, Whom did I know, or whom was I visiting? When they learned that I neither knew nor was visiting anyone, most interviews ended on the spot—even though most people had promised at church to offer their assistance.

Quite by coincidence, I gave an elderly lady a ride to Charleston. As I drove along the winding roads, she told me that she lived alone, loved to crab and fish, and took a "nip" for her arthritis every now and then. She had lived in the Wadmalaw community all her life and had a host of relatives and friends on neighboring islands up and down the Carolina/Georgia coast. She knew the traditions; later, she would be instrumental in helping me to learn them. Because this lady was socially active and was held in high esteem, she was ultimately able to provide me with acceptable answers to the questions Sea Islanders ask of all new faces. I became Miss Myma's "granddaughter" who lived away and came to visit every summer.[1] (My greatest accomplishment would be finally getting her to leave Wadmalaw and come to Michigan to visit me.)

Having a person well known and well respected to provide a lineage helped in my approaches to the community. But since most people born on any given island know each other, I soon realized that I had the status of "outsider," and no outsiders, black or white, are welcomed warmly into Sea Island activities or viewed without suspicion until they have spent considerable time among the people, performing daily tasks and becoming involved in daily living activities. The people have long been ridiculed for their speech, life-style, and mannerisms. In addition, they are very much aware that their culture has been a topic of interest to folklorists, linguists, historians, and others since the early twentieth century.[2] Thus they are quite naturally suspicious of anyone taking notes, carrying equipment, or wandering about unaccompanied by a resident. The islanders are a proud, perceptive people and can very soon sense insincerity and patronizing attitudes. It generally requires more than an offer of cash payment, gifts, or other remunerations to motivate them to assist a researcher's study. Though it was not my original plan to become indoctrinated into Sea Island culture through hard labor, I learned very quickly that most of the islanders are active, "going" people. Those who are not engaged in city jobs are likely to be fishermen, farmers, carpenters, housewives, basket weavers, market people, or laborers in the produce fields. Often workers allowed me to accompany and assist them, and I found that the rewards for becoming involved in daily life through hard work were great indeed. Returning home from a day in the fields in an open-bed truck, listening to the islanders laughing, joking, and planning for the weekend, made the tasks I had accomplished that day seem easier. Equally important, I obtained some of the most interesting speech data while learning to make baskets or working in an okra field.

After five years of gathering information on the Sea Islands, I went to Africa in 1978 to compare the Sea Islanders' language and culture with the patterns of some of their ancestors. The Nigerian villagers' welcome was far warmer on my first introduction to their communities than the Sea Islanders' had been. Many of the elderly Igbo, Yoruba, and Ibebio women had never seen an African-American woman and walked some distances to see the *Indocha,* or what was termed a "white-black woman." The label was used not out of disrespect but for lack of a better one to refer to a person born from African heritage but raised speaking a European tongue. After I explained my purpose for coming far "across the water," I was never in need of anyone to assist in any efforts. The villagers were as eager to hear what words, customs, and traditions the Gullah speakers retained as I was to tell them. Their eagerness was sharpened by their fervent hope that somehow some of the language, literary traditions, and social customs had derived from their particular culture, whether Igbo, Yoruba, or Ibebio. Life among these people was fascinating and amazingly similar in some ways to the life patterns of the Sea Islanders, even after the passage of centuries. It is about these similarities in language, literature, and culture that I promised to write this book.

# 1

## The Social History and Organization

Me old building e de leak,
and me soul e got fe move:

*There is a leak in this old building (body),*
*and my soul has got to move:*


### Topography

The Sea Islands, commonly known as the Gullah- or Geechee-speaking communities, extend along the coast of South Carolina and Georgia to the tip of Florida. Isolated by expansive marshlands, turbulent streams, and massive rivers, some islands are several miles from the coast of the United States. Estimates indicate that there are as many as a thousand islands along the coastline, though many of them are small and unfit for human habitation.[1] The habitable ones vary in size. St. Helena, for example, covers only 15 square miles, while Wadmalaw extends for 43. Sandy Island, still not connected by bridge to the mainland, is estimated to be 50 square miles; Edisto is about 72; and Johns Island, the second largest island in U.S. waters, is approximately 100.[2]

The Sea Islands of South Carolina, on which most of this study is based, extend on the north from Sandy Island near Georgetown to Port Royal, St. Helena, and Daufuski on the south. Sandy Island is traditionally included among the Sea Islands of South Carolina because it is culturally similar to the coastal islands; it is, however, a freshwater river island rather than a saltwater ocean island.[3] The islands just off the coast of Charleston include James, Johns, Wadmalaw, Edisto, and Yonges, among many others. The Sea Islands of Georgia extend on the northern coast from Harris Neck; on the southern coast they include Sapelo, Darien, St. Simons, and St. Marys.

The Sea Islands and surrounding areas were a mere submerged portion of the continental shelf during the early geologic history of North America. As time passed, the ocean retreated to its present position, and the low flatlands left behind became known as the Georgia and Carolina low country.[4]

The Sea Islands are tranquil, flat, swampy lands with elevations ranging from near sea level to slightly over 100 feet. The climate is generally mild throughout the year, with very few recordings of drastically low temperatures. The coastal areas are characterized by slightly higher annual temperatures than other areas, primarily because of their proximity to the ocean.[5] The climatogram shown in Figure 1 illustrates the changes at various times of the year.

The Sea Island area is characterized by deep rivers snaking along the coast and dividing the land into countless large and small islands. The sandy soil, which drains inadequately, places economic and developmental constraints on the area. Road building is extremely difficult in spots; some islands still have no paved roads. The 1979 regional housing market analysis for the Berkeley-Charleston-Dorchester (BCD) Council of Governments estimated that 90 percent of the land area within Charleston County, which includes many of the Carolina Sea Islands, is composed of soils that put moderate to severe limitations on land use for urban development. The soil has poor load-bearing capacities, in addition to the prevailing poor drainage. Thus, financing for development must include provisions for land improvement as well as adequate drainage systems. Of the 2,614 square miles of land within the BCD region, only 5 percent has been developed for urban use; remaining portions of the coastal region are primarily rural.[6] Slightly more than half of the area is forest and woodlands. The marsh and swamplands, nearly a quarter of the total, grow little but marsh weeds, owing to the ebb and flow of daily tidal waters. These lands are flat and dangerous; there are reports of unfortunate islanders' being caught in "suckholes" or "mashmud" and never returning. The overall pattern of land use is summarized in Table 1.

Few bridges, with the exception of wooden crossings, connected

Figure 1. Climatic Overview of the Sea Islands and Adjacent Coastal
Areas

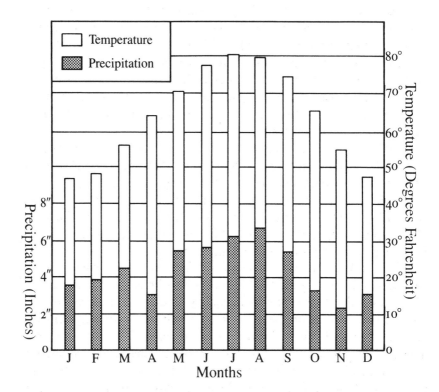

Rainfall is moderate, averaging about 50 inches per year. The temperature throughout the region
usually ranges from 45 to 80 degrees Fahrenheit; the recorded extremes are 2 and 103 degrees
Fahrenheit. *Source:* Waccamaw Regional Planning and Development Council, *Waccamaw
Regional Housing Element,* 1977, p. 8.

Table 1. Land Use for BCD Region

| Category | Acres | % of Total |
|---|---|---|
| Developed areas | | |
|   Urban uses | 75,000 | 4.29 |
|     Residential | 21,000 | 1.20 |
|     Commercial | 3,500 | 0.20 |
|     Industrial | 12,600 | 0.72 |
|     Public and other | 37,900 | 2.17 |
|   Agricultural uses | | |
|     Cropland and pasture | 178,800 | 10.23 |
|     Forest and woodlands | 861,740 | 49.30 |
|       (excluding swampland forests) | | |
| Undeveloped areas | | |
|   Marsh and swampland | 416,600 | 23.83 |
|   Inland waterways | 140,800 | 8.06 |
| Total | 1,747,940 | 100.00 |

Source: BCD Council of Governments, *Regional Housing Market Analysis,* 1975, p. 5; figuring corrected.

the islands to the mainland before 1940. Though considerable sums of money have been expended within recent years on the construction of long, narrow bridges to span the Atlantic coast, ocean recesses, rivers, and streams, the more remote islands, such as Sandy and Daufuski, continue to be inaccessible except by boat.[7] Most of the Sea Islands remain very sparsely settled despite the population growth brought on by recent industrialization and commercialization. The landscape is pastoral and mysterious compared to inland areas of the United States. Most islands are characterized by graceful palmetto trees, expansive green terrain, and atmospheric haze. The landscape in fact bears a striking resemblance to the topography of such coastal countries as Nigeria, Ghana, Angola, and Liberia, the tropical homelands of the Sea Islanders' ancestors.[8]

Electricity came to the more remote islands only as recently as the 1960s. Streetlights rarely line the narrow roadways of even the more developed islands, and in late evening the overhanging trees give the roads a ghostly allure. After nightfall it is literally impossible to see even two feet ahead.[9]

The main roadways branch into dozens of dirt roads angling around bends, across creeks, and through narrow passageways before leading to small communities. As remote as some homes are, many are large, fully equipped, and constructed of brick or wood with aluminum siding. These homes reflect modernization, improved education, and the rise of a younger, more affluent island society. Yet nestled amid these relatively expensive new homes are ancient, two-roomed houses, gray and weather-beaten but standing firm on the wooden blocks that have supported them for as much as a century and a half. These houses are called "shanties" by the islanders and are most often occupied by the oldest members of the community. Because islanders believe that the human breath is the primary factor in preserving a dwelling place, even a young family will sometimes prefer living in a shanty which has been recently occupied to living in a newer, larger home which has been vacated for a long time. Most shanties are kept neat and orderly—a remarkable housekeeping achievement, because as many as ten people may occupy one of these tiny older homes.

In addition to the modern homes and the shanties, trailer homes are common on the Sea Islands, especially on islands with no bridges connecting them to the coast. The trailer homes are convenient and economical. They generally come fully equipped with modern conveniences, and they can be easily dismantled, loaded onto a barge, and floated to an island.

Many of the older and some of the newer island homes are built to share a common yard area, which is kept free of grass and litter and is swept as part of the daily care. Maintaining a communal dirt yard was once routine for black families in the South, and it is also traditional in most West African villages. Even members of some of the most affluent African families, with expensive eight-bedroom homes, magnificent by any standard, keep the yard area completely free of grass by morning and afternoon sweepings. This smooth yard is functional on the Sea Islands as well as in Africa: keeping it grassless helps to eliminate insects and provides a clean, unlittered surface where children can play and elders can congregate to smoke, talk, and drink palm wine. This communal yard was the primary place where I was taken both on the Sea Islands and in Africa to listen to folktales and singing.

## Demography

The Sea Islands were the homes of Indians before the Europeans and Africans came to America, and thus the region is characterized by names like Wadmalaw, Sampit, Santee, Yamassee, Pee Dee,
Winyah, Waccamaw, and Yacamaw. After the forced migration in the
early 1700s of the Yamassee and other Indians, the coastal islands
became the home of African slaves, a few white planters, and ex-slaves
and their free descendants.[10] Not many whites or Europeans inhabited
the islands during the slave trade, and in some places white permanent
residents are still rare.[11] Federal census figures for the coastal areas
have until very recently shown high concentrations of African and
African-American populations. For example, 1830 figures revealed an
overwhelmingly black population. The Georgetown district of South
Carolina at that time contained 1,940 whites and 18,000 blacks. A
grand jury presentment held during the fall term of 1835 complained
that the black-to-white ratio in Georgetown was becoming unwieldy
and insisted that something had to be done. Noting that 10 masters of
1,700 slaves were permanently absent from their property, the jury
went on to object that there were only 40 proprietors to oversee a black
population of 15,000 on the Tide Swamp plantation.[12] On many of the
islands the only white persons present were the owners, and in many
cases there was no overseer.[13]

In 1798 the Georgia Constitution prohibited direct slave importation from Africa, and the Constitution of the United States made the
slave trade illegal after 1808. Nevertheless, the navigable ocean recesses of the islands and the turbulent rivers leading miles into the
interior facilitated the landing of slaves brought directly from Africa.
Slave trading thus continued to flourish in the coastal region as late as
1858, when the slave ship *Wanderer* brought new slaves to the Georgia
coast. By this time inland parts of the United States were sufficiently
supplied with generations of native-born African-Americans, so the
coastal cities and the Sea Islands absorbed the newly arrived African
population. The continued addition of Africans to communities with
few, if any, Europeans and an already dense African population made
possible the reinforcement and perpetuation of African traditions in
these areas.[14]

By 1880 the federal census revealed that Charleston County contained 30,922 whites and 71,868 blacks. By 1940 the Sea Island communities still maintained a majority black population. The 1940 census for Johns Island, South Carolina, revealed that of the 3,534 residents of the island, 2,623 were black. On Wadmalaw Island, where many of the data for this study were collected, only 251 of the 1,607 inhabitants in 1940 were white. The black-to-white ratio of Charleston County and the surrounding Sea Islands remained fairly stable until the late 1930s and the 1940s. The BCD Council of Governments records that between 1930 and 1970 Charleston County witnessed a 145% population increase, with further increments of approximately 4,200 persons per year between 1970 and 1978. This population growth is largely attributed to the increasing industrialization and commercialization brought by the new bridges connecting many of the islands to the coast. Most of the immigration since 1930 has been by whites. The 1970 census indicated that blacks constituted only 31.4 percent of the population of Charleston County, compared to more than 50 percent in 1930.[15]

While this distribution does reflect a major change in racial composition, especially in the Charleston County area during the last 100 or more years, the demographic picture of the Sea Islands is somewhat obscured by the distribution of the new arrivals. Only a few of the Sea Islands have experienced major changes in population and industrialization, and these are not among the most remote and economically distressed areas. Unemployment and population lag seem to be related to remoteness: islands with adequate bridges and paved roadways that provide excellent access to and from the Charleston area, like James and Johns in South Carolina, are undergoing significant population growth, as is shown in Table 2.

The population growth for the Johns Island Division is due to major commercialization and to developmental pressures from the exclusive resort construction still occurring on Kiawah and Seabrook Islands, which are a part of the division (see Appendix 4). James Island, situated just over the bridge from Charleston, is highly urbanized and is one of the major arteries to the Folly Beach area. The new inhabitants in both island divisions, as elsewhere, are primarily white. Whereas blacks constituted approximately 80 percent of the total population of the Johns Island township in 1940, only 41 percent of the island residents were black in 1970, and that ratio remained relatively stable through 1980.[16]

As the data in Table 2 indicate, Wadmalaw and Edisto, com-

Table 2. Racial Breakdowns for Five of the Carolina Sea Islands

| Year | Population | Edisto | James | Johns | Wadmalaw | St. Helena |
|------|-----------|--------|-------|-------|----------|-----------|
| 1930 | Total | 1,948 | 3,058 | 3,264 | 2,054 | 4,626 |
|      | Black | 1,693 | 2,419 | 2,826 | 1,813 | 4,458 |
| 1940 | Total | 1,955 | 3,913 | 3,534 | 1,858 | 4,266 |
|      | Black | 1,717 | 2,709 | 2,633 | 1,607 | 3,961 |
| 1960 | Total | 1,589 | 13,872 | 6,252 | 2,326 | 6,048 |
|      | Black | 1,306 | 4,168 | 3,260 | 1,980 | 4,994 |
| 1970 | Total | 1,374 | 18,969 | 7,530 | 2,024 | 5,718 |
|      | Black | 1,115 | 5,217 | 3,104 | 1,719 | 4,278 |
| 1980 | Total | 1,345 | 27,719 | 9,296 | 2,440 | 8,134 |
|      | Black | 1,124 | 6,173 | 3,975 | 1,935 | 4,934 |

*Source:* U.S. censuses of population.

paratively remote, do not show any significant population changes. In the late 1970s Edisto Island had only 19 persons per square mile dispersed over a 72.6-square-mile land area. The 1980 census revealed a population of 1,345 persons—another slight decrease. Edisto's population remains predominantly black (84 percent). Its slow growth is attributed to the lack of incorporated areas, of major manufacturers, and of essential services such as water and sewer.[17]

Wadmalaw Island, situated between Johns and Edisto, is rural in nature and like Edisto has exhibited very little in- or out-migration. In 1970, 85 percent of the people were black, and this figure had dropped only to 79 percent in 1980. Even though 80 percent of the housing is occupied by owners, Wadmalaw is ranked second in the region in economic distress. It has no water or sewer services, and its only industry is Metal Trades, which provides services primarily for ship repair. Most of the inhabitants are laborers, farmers, and fishermen, though there are an increasing number of professional persons who have returned home to the island to work as doctors, lawyers, teachers, and so on.[18]

The addition of more whites is not precipitating an erosion of the traditional social and racial composition of most of the Sea Island communities. They remain isolated, with predominantly black populations. Only the most readily accessible islands, particularly James,

Table 3. Population Projection for Charleston County

|  | 1970 | 1975 | 1980 | 1985 | 1990 | 1995 |
|---|---|---|---|---|---|---|
| Edisto Island | 1,374 | 1,170 | 1,120 | 1,110 | 1,150 | 1,190 |
| James Island | 24,197 | 25,944 | 29,280 | 33,064 | 36,890 | 40,450 |
| Johns Island | 7,530 | 8,853 | 10,483 | 12,016 | 13,469 | 14,999 |
| McClellanville* | 4,094 | 3,867 | 3,814 | 3,905 | 3,994 | 4,125 |
| Wadmalaw Island | 2,024 | 1,900 | 2,150 | 2,250 | 2,450 | 2,650 |

*Source:* BCD Council of Governments *Regional Housing Market Analysis,* 1979, p. 21.
*McClellanville is not a Sea Island. It is included here because it is a coastal city that has always had a concentration of African-Americans, most of whom do speak a variety of Gullah.

Johns, Kiawah, and Seabrook, have undergone significant population changes in the recent past (see Table 3).

## Economy

In the past, the Sea Islanders depended on agriculture and their natural environment for survival. Without a doubt, the new job opportunities brought to some of the islands by industry and commerce will affect this pattern. In fact, current census data indicate that farming is already being abandoned in exchange for more lucrative livelihoods. By 1970 only 10 percent of the people on Johns Island and 15 percent of those on Wadmalaw were farmers. The figures for farm laborers were 13.4 percent on Johns, 20.8 percent on Wadmalaw. The Kiawah Island Company painted a glowing picture of the employment opportunities that the resort could offer to area residents, estimating that "operating employment for the resort would range from 476 to 511 in 1976, increase yearly to a range of 1,227 to 1,473 by 1980, and climb to an incredible 4,034 to 4,458 jobs by 1990." Although the company's figures have proved thus far to be somewhat optimistic, the resort development has indeed provided jobs for Sea Islanders:

> On Kiawah Island, blacks from Johns, Wadmalaw, and other areas have recently received both construction and operations jobs, although the skill levels these jobs involve are either fairly high or fairly low. Kiawah estimates, for example, that in August of 1976

there were 181 construction workers on their island, and 38 or 40 percent of those were black, although all did not come from the immediate area. In the area of operations employment, 111 of 250 total workers on Kiawah or 44 percent were from Johns, Wadmalaw, or Yonges in April of 1976. These are startup operations, but the same trends can be observed on Hilton Head Island. At the Hilton Head Company, 37 of the 103 workers are minorities, as compared to 40 percent local residents as employees for the local Holiday Inn.[19]

Despite these improved job opportunities, the Sea Islands remain among areas listed by the BCD Council of Governments as economically distressed. For example, Edisto Island had a 1970 median family income of about $2,500. Approximately 60 percent of Edisto's population reported incomes below the 1970 poverty level. Of the 2,024 residents on Wadmalaw Island, 1,053 had incomes below the poverty level; the median income for Wadmalaw was $4,700.[20]

The high poverty levels reported for the Sea Island areas are related not so much to the employment opportunities in the area as to a lack of skills that prevents the islanders from applying for well-paid jobs. In 1980 more than 50 percent of the respondents in one study undertaken on Wadmalaw, Johns, and James islands had less than a ninth-grade education (though there are many permanent inhabitants of the Sea Islands who hold university and professional degrees). Members of the labor force in 1980 were employed as unskilled private household workers, maintenance workers, clerks, food service workers, unskilled hospital personnel, and the like.[21]

As noted, the agricultural patterns have changed over the years. When the Indians had been driven out of the islands, the land was owned partly by tenant black farmers and partly by white planters whose acreage was worked by African slaves. Immediately after the Civil War, only blacks could buy land in the region. Thousands of acres had been left by planters when they fled from the Union troops. They could not buy back the land because they could not pay the federal direct tax imposed by the Washington government, and even if they had been financially able to pay the taxes, they could not have made their way through the Union camps to do so. The federal government and various societies in the North wishing to befriend the blacks wanted the island property to go to the free slaves. To meet this intention, General W. T. Sherman issued his famous Field Order No. 15: "The islands from Charleston, south, the abandoned rice fields along the rivers for thirty miles back from the sea, and the country bordering the St. Johns river, Florida, are reserved and set apart for the settlement of the Negroes."[22]

From the earliest days the islanders tended to be self-sufficient agriculturally. The landowners—black or white—harvested mainly indigo and long-staple cotton, commodities that thrived well on the rich island soil. Rice, by 1724 one of the most profitable staple commodities in the mainland coastal areas,[23] was not grown to any great extent on the islands.[24]

Peter Wood writes convincingly that the West Africans were primarily responsible for the economic success of the flourishing rice crops in the Carolina territory. The cultivation, growth, and processing of rice is an old tradition in West Africa. During the eighteenth and nineteenth centuries rice was grown in most West African areas, and especially heavily near the Gambia River. In the Congo-Angola region, a white explorer once noted that rice was so plentiful that it brought no price at all. During this period West Africans actually sold rice to the slave traders to stock their ships.[25]

Unlike the Europeans, then, who knew little about rice, the transplanted Africans were widely familiar with its cultivation. In fact, rice was so important a part of African culture that its growth and harvest were celebrated each year, just as the growing of yams was celebrated in "yam festivals."[26] In West Africa today there is still a kind of symbolism associated with rice and yams: they are much more than just food to be consumed.[27] Rice continues to be a primary food in both West Africa and the Sea Islands, and its preparation and offering tend to be expressions of fine taste and "good eating."[28]

Until recent years the primary Sea Island commodity was long-staple cotton, a crop that thrives only in light, sandy, saltwater lands. Because of its fine silky texture, it brought excellent prices on the world market, and it was grown along the Atlantic coast from the Santee River of South Carolina to the Florida Everglades.[29] The rapid expansion of cotton production on the islands, as elsewhere, was a major factor in the great demand for West African slaves to work the fields. Perhaps because cotton was a crop new to the slaves, or because the growth and harvest of an inedible crop did not offer the familiar gratification associated with rice, or merely because of the connection with slavery, the mention of cotton in Sea Island folklore and literature generally has negative connotations.

Today neither cotton nor rice is grown to any extent on or around the Sea Islands. Rice was gradually eliminated by the many disastrous floods and storms which frequent the Carolina coast. Cotton was abandoned in favor of more lucrative means of support, especially since the cotton-picking machine eliminated the need for harvesting of cotton by hand. The primary crops now are edible produce, including soybeans, peas, okra, tomatoes, corn, peanuts, and watermelons, and many folk narratives focus on the planting, cultivation, and harvesting of these crops.

Another major food source is fish, shrimp, crabs, oysters, mussels, clams, lobsters, conchs, and sharks, all of which the islanders prepare expertly and variously. Fish has always been important in the local diet. Consider, for example, a resident minister's account of the varieties available around Edisto Island in 1800:

> The creeks, rivers, and seas which indent and surround the island furnish at different and appropriate seasons of the year, a great variety of excellent fish—as the larger drum, the small black drum, bass, rock-fish, sheephead, cavallie, bonnetta, salmon-trout, yellowtail, ale-wife, croaker, plaice, flounder, skate, pike, shad, and catfish, and many others, suitable for the table. Porpoise and sharks frequent the creeks and surrounding waters. Some of the latter are seen and caught of an enormous size. They are considered as just objects of terror by the negroes. And yet, although the fishermen continue hours together waist deep in water, and have often the misfortune of hooking them, they escape with impunity.[30]

Crabbing and fishing are so much a part of Sea Island culture that many children learn the fine art of casting and netting as early as three years old. Some residents who earn their livings from fishing practice an old African method of netting fish in mass. An elderly gentleman explained to me that his grandfather had taught him to beat on the sides of his boat to attract fish and porpoises to the area (see Appendix 1). The porpoises scare schools of fish ahead of them, and the fish are then caught in the nets. In a variant of this method, a group of fishermen will wade out into the water to beat on their drums or other instruments. The more noise they create above and below water, the more fish they attract to the area. One has to be careful in this venture, however, because the drums may also bring sharks.[31]

Though much sustenance is taken from the rivers, the streams, and the ocean, another food source is provided by creatures that live at the edge of the water, such as "cooters" (slider turtles), bullfrogs, terrapins, alligators, and sometimes rattlesnakes (not everyone will eat the latter because the flesh is believed to be poisonous if the snake was angered before it was killed). The flesh from the cooter is particularly pleasing to some islanders owing to its unusual taste and tender texture. The alligator is a rare delicacy, now, being no longer as readily available as it was in the past. Yet Ber Gator[32] and his swampy home continue to be lively topics in folklore and literature. Under the slave regime, according to one source, when the islanders were denied the use of guns and powder, they hunted the alligator armed only with a long hook. They entered his hole at low tide and, at considerable risk to their lives and legs, dragged the alligator out and killed him quickly. The skin was saved to sell and the flesh taken home for cooking.[33]

This dangerous method of hunting alligators is reminiscent of an even more dangerous method once used to trap the giant boa constrictors and pythons in Nigeria. One Igbo hunter explained to me that the snake hunters rubbed their bodies with a scent taken from captured boa constrictors and pythons before entering places which they were known to inhabit, in order to prevent the snake from smelling their approach. Once the quarry's hole had been located, either the hunters dragged him out with a hook or, at greater risk, one man would insert a leg into the snake's hole, allowing the snake to swallow it up to the hip. When the leg was pulled out the snake came along helplessly, unable to move with the hunter's leg in his mouth. The hunter quickly drew his knife, slit the snake's jaws and throat, and thus recovered his leg. The account of this method of hunting was corroborated by some Nigerians and called a lie by others. The hunter who told me about it, however, swore that it was indeed done. Like the alligators in the United States, the giant snakes are captured in Nigeria chiefly for their hides. The larger the snake, the more dangerous his capture is, and thus the greater the price paid for his skin will be.

The woods provide a further excellent supply of food for the Sea Islanders. Many of the more remote islands still abound with large ducks, partridges, wild turkeys, geese, and many other edible birds. Likewise, the woodlands are alive with game. Deer often roam alongside the roads in the early morning. Opossums are baked with large sweet potatoes, and raccoons are delicacies no islander will refuse. The woods are also the home of rabbits, wolves, foxes, squirrels, skunks, wildcats, and even bears, all hunted, though bears are said to be rather rare now. The islanders have generally been able to rely on a variety of wild game. One seventeenth-century explorer compiled a list:

> Deer, of which there is such infinite Herds, that the whole Country seems but one continued Park, insomuch that I have often heard Captain Matthew, an ingenious Gentleman an Agent to Sir Peter Colleton for his Affairs in Carolina, say that one hunting Indian had yearly kill'd and brought to his Plantation more than 100, sometimes 200 head of Deer. Bears there are in great numbers. . . . There are Bevors, Otters, Foxes, Raccoons, Possums, Musquasses, Hare and Coneys, Squirrels of five kinds, the flying squirrel, whose delicate skin is commended for comforting, if applied to a cold Stomach, the Red, the Grey, the Fox and Black Squirrels.[34]

The islanders, old and young, are fully acquainted with the ways of the local wild animals. Their partial dependency on these animals as a food source has caused them to pay closer attention to the animals' personalities and habits than would a hunter from another area. Thus their categorization of the animals into intelligent and not-so-intelligent ones is based on day-to-day interaction.[35]

In addition to relying on the natural environment,[36] many islanders continue an economic practice which is still the primary method of consumer exchange in the homelands of their ancestors, selling crafts and services along with their game and farm produce. Individual island families are known for "growing" carpenters, tailors, shoemakers, butchers, cabinetmakers, hairdressers, candlemakers, brickmasons, builders, farmers, ministers, and herbalists (or "rootmen"). Family members tend to follow the traditions set by preceding members of the family and handed down from generation to generation. The old skills brought from Africa or learned during slavery, when everything needed for the plantation was made or serviced by the slaves,[37] have lingered in the protected environment of the Sea Islands. Among the skills highly valued on the islands are carpentry, masonry, and the like—essential because the remoteness of the islands means that most of the homes have to be built by the islanders themselves.

The Sea Island crafts—jewelry, pottery, fans, baskets—often reflect African styles. Basketry is one of the dominant crafts of the region, and one of the oldest crafts of African origin in the United States. The baskets were originally made for practical purposes: winnowing rice, carrying clothing, cradling infants, fanning, sorting foods. These were called work baskets and were made of sturdy weaves and such materials as bulrushes and palmetto butts. While the basket weavers still make work baskets, they find that most customers are more interested in their "show baskets," which are lighter and more colorful but less sturdy and sometimes less expensive to make. The show baskets have various designs, ranging from a tiny candle holder to a gigantic woven bin. Whereas the work baskets are relics of the African utility traditions, the show pieces, including purses, vases, and glasses trays, show European influences and are usually decorative in intent. Within recent years the basket weavers of Mt. Pleasant, a town on the South Carolina coast, have gained fame for their skills with the traditional designs. Their baskets are displayed in educational centers and museums of art throughout the United States and elsewhere, and are purchased by art collectors the world over as survivals of an ancient African craft.

Various observers have compared the baskets of the South Carolina coast with their African counterparts. According to one knowledgeable collector, there are strong technical links in weave pattern, design, and final product between the Carolina flat and fanner baskets and those of Nigeria, Togo, Benin, and Ghana.[38] The Sea Island coiling technique, the manner of stitching, and the pattern of functional use within an agricultural framework have been likened to the style of Senegal, though coiling, an old and widespread technique, is not by itself sufficient to identify an African source.[39] Given that similarities in technique and style may be misleading, the deciding factor in comparisons is the cultural milieu of which the baskets are a part. Because Africans were transplanted from the Gold Coast to America, and because Sea Island African-Americans continue to make baskets that are so like the African counterparts that it is almost impossible to differentiate them, it seems reasonable to accept the fact of a historical link.[40]

Children, both boys and girls, are taught basketmaking along with the other traditional skills. Boys and men most often gather mate-

Children learn the art of basketmaking at an early age.

Miss Mary practices her ancient craft.

rials—pine needles, bulrushes, sweet grass, and palmetto leaves—for the girls and women to weave. The children learn to make baskets at around six years of age, and by the time they are in their teens, each has mastered a certain style and design that generally carries his or her trademark in the weave. Most of the baskets follow a simple coiling technique with a knot used as a base. The free ends of the sweet grass bundle are folded and then wound around the knot to begin a coil. Then an opening is pierced in the center knot and a strip of palm leaf is pulled through the opening, wrapped around the grass coil, and pulled back through a second opening made in the knot to anchor or station the coil. As this process is repeated, the coil begins to circle out from the center knot to create a basket base that is circular or oval. From this base, the basket is constructed by changing the angle at which one circular row is fastened to another. The palm stitch in the Mt. Pleasant baskets does not interlock with the stitches in previous rows of the coil. Consequently, the stitches appear to radiate out from the center knot in a linear way, much like the spokes of a wheel.[41]

The baskets, like the islanders' other crafts, are displayed along U.S. Highway 17, north of Charleston, or sold in the open markets near downtown Charleston where tourists crowd in daily to haggle over the prices of vegetables, hand-woven clothing, jewelry, and other wares, including items of brass, silver, and gold. Everything has a bargain price, and the basket sellers, like the other marketeers, are professionals in the art of bargaining. Baskets are priced according to size and difficulty of design, and it is a bad reflection on one's selling skills to be pressured into parting with a basket at a price lower than that established by the community; such an act may bring censure from one's family and from members of the community. The basket weavers, although seemingly unsophisticated and some of them certainly poor, are quite shrewd bargainers. I watched an exchange that took place when a very impressive car stopped in front of a basket stand along Highway 17. The driver, smoking a large cigar and accompanied by three elegantly dressed women, strolled over to look at the baskets. He picked up a tray of coasters and asked the basket weaver how much she would charge him to make coasters with specific dimensions for his beer cans. She hesitated, looked down at the basket that she was weaving, and said, "About twenty dollars." He then asked how long it would take for her to make them. She replied with some reservation that it would take her at least a week. He quickly took a twenty-dollar bill from his wallet, tore it in half, gave her half of it, and told her he would give her the other half when she finished weaving the coasters. He left thinking that he had indeed made a bargain. Feeling somewhat dismayed by the whole procedure, I asked her how she could afford to make the coasters for only twenty dollars if it took her a week to weave them. She smiled slyly and said she could make them in a matter of hours.

## Social Structure

The ways of the Sea Islanders, as I have said, offer valuable insights into an Afro-American culture which has had relatively little contact with the customs of the white majority until very recent years. According to one group of researchers, the unusual circumstances which created the culture also "created a unique psyche for Blacks in the Sea Island area":

> We have seen their consequences in a number of ways in our re-search. We constantly encounter elderly Blacks whose knowledge of and acquaintance with whites is very limited. They have not had to interact with whites or the majority culture in the same way as Blacks in the other parts of this country. Many of them have a fierce kind of pride and a lack of fear which is seldom seen in other places. The self-doubt and sense of inadequacy and inferiority often cited as characteristic of the Black psyche are not found to the same degrees in our Sea Island research.[42]

Their preserved traditions, too, set the Sea Islanders apart from other Americans, black or white. The extended family is the norm in the Sea Islands. Most islands are sectioned off into family communities, where all members of one family, their close relatives, and people remotely related live or have a right to live as long as they can satisfactorily show evidence of kinship. Land is not normally sold to family members but is passed on through an unwritten contract called "heir's land"; if land *is* sold to relatives, the charge is only one dollar to fulfill "legal tenets of the state."[43]

Land ownership is closely aligned with kinship, and kinship is the primary social factor necessary for acceptance into island communities. One must be born, reared, and have a known family history on a given island in order to be accepted as a natural member of the community. Members who are brought to the islands as spouses are recognized as members by association with a known island family, but even one who has been married to an islander for twenty or more years never achieves the status of a full member of the community.

Membership is most often established through oral transmission of lineage, as opposed to birth certificates or other documents. Thus one is expected to know one's lineage, for this knowledge can mean the difference between acceptance and rejection in any social setting. It is normal protocol, for example, for a young person to undergo seemingly intense interrogation by an older island resident who wishes to place the younger person. If one can explain satisfactorily who one's parents are, who one's parents' parents are, or even who one's cousins' parents are, then kinship is established and one is viewed as a member of the community to be accorded all due warmth and hospitality. The islanders can be chilly and sometimes openly hostile to strangers, black or white, who have no local kinship ties or affiliations.

As would be expected in such closed communities, familial ties, marriages, and the concept of the extended family are taken with utmost seriousness. The extended family is an African-like social tradition on the Sea Islands, just as it is in most inland black communities; acknowledging and readily accepting the obligations and responsibilities due not only to one's spouse but also to one's spouse's family is a part of island culture. The "conjugal bond is strong and literally lasts until death parts the spouses," and common-law marriages are as valid and stable in the eyes of the community as those marriages contracted under law. There is a low incidence of divorce and separation. Disagreements and conflicts do arise in Sea Island households, of course, as they do in any household. But understanding and accepting the relationships inherited in an extended family appear to alleviate many of the conflicts experienced in the sort of nuclear family that is characteristic of European cultures, such as mother-in-law/daughter-in-law antagonism. Like the members of extended families in Africa, people on the Sea Islands act with deference toward their elders, and most elders accord a great degree of respect to young adults, especially those with children. That is, conflicts are minimized because each member acknowledges and respects the others' domains.[44]

Most of the inhabitants of any given island are related; thus marriage between persons from the same island is not encouraged. Children are expected from Sea Island marriages, whether they are the couple's own or just living with them. Children are highly prized regardless of the financial condition of the parents, and abortion is rare and generally viewed as an abomination against God and nature. If a young couple joins a parent's household, rather than establishing a new one, the elder members of the family usually take responsibility for the care and discipline of the children. Many elderly residents, the guardians of several generations of children, attribute their longevity and good health to the belief that they *cannot* die until all the children for whom they are responsible are grown and able to care for themselves, or until their responsibilities are delegated to someone else. Some children are reared by sisters, aunts, uncles, or even distant cousins. It is not unusual for a child to reach adulthood living not more than a block from the natural parent but residing with another relative, who is perhaps childless or more financially secure. Even children born out of wedlock generally know who their fathers and grandparents are. These children are given the same respect in the community as legitimate children and are as likely to be reared by the paternal side of the family as by the maternal side.[45]

The church is probably the most important social organization in the Sea Island communities. Outwardly, the Sunday services follow the patterns prescribed for Baptist and Methodist churches and are thus based on Christian doctrine. Some of the beliefs of black Christians in the Sea Islands are quite distinctive. For example, I have heard many elderly residents speak of a tripartite division of the human being into body, soul, and spirit, whereas Christian doctrine teaches that a person has only a body and a soul which is synonymous with the spirit. According to many elderly island residents, when one dies, only the soul returns to the kingdom of God. The body and spirit remain on earth. And although the soul of the dead person cannot harm the living, the spirit can, at will, cause another to harm him- or herself.[46]

This concept of a tripartite body, soul, and spirit, with the body and spirit remaining on earth after death and able to influence the living, is widespread in West Africa today. Many African peoples do not conceive of any geographical separation between the real world and the spirit world; as soon as the body dies physically, they believe the person arrives in the spirit world.[47] To these physical and spiritual entities, some societies add a belief in a "shadow" entity.[48] The Sea

Islanders have delineated this three-part concept very precisely. It was
described to me by a very religious Sea Island man as follows:

> Listen to me good now: when you die in this world, you see,
> the . . . the . . . the . . . soul of a man go home to the Kingdom
> of God, but your spirit still's here on earth. . . .And if you
> was . . . the devil in all your days . . . your spirit, after you
> dead, your spirit can do the same thing. Your soul up there, but
> your spirit de right down de here with the body. . . . And that's
> the one gone . . . gone do the effect to you. You see now . . .
> now that's, that's why I say this now. A lot of people don't
> believe. Say, say . . . say is not ghost. Is ghost there.

The "dream spirit," this man continued, must be permitted periodi-
cally to take leave of the body and roam. It therefore leaves the body
and wanders all over the world when one goes to sleep. The body is
unprotected while the spirit is away, however, and if the spirit should
come in contact with a second, evil spirit while it is roaming, it must
race back to the body. When this happens, the person may cry out in
sleep and become frightened; if the spirit does not come back to the
body, the person dies in sleep.[49]

Another distinctive element in the islanders' world view is their
belief in voodoo, or hoodoo. This belief involves rituals whereby spirits, good or evil, are conjured up to offer predictions, kill enemies, or
perform cures for problems ranging from broken hearts, infertility, and
rheumatism to mental illness and cancer. The spirit of one's ancestors
is considered the closest link to the spirits of the "other" world. Thus,
on the Sea Islands as well as in Africa, spirits are asked to intervene on
behalf of a living relative. The belief in voodoo is still so strong in the
Sea Island area that Dr. Buzzard, a known practitioner of the occult,
maintained a high standard of living from reading signs, effecting certain cures, and appealing to the spirits.

The islanders set great store on preparation for burial and consider
it an abomination to die without having made the necessary financial
arrangements to be buried at home. Thus some islanders pay on burial
policies all of their lives. By tradition a parent starts a burial policy for
each child that is born, paying twenty-five to fifty cents per month until
the policy is paid in full. It may take one's whole life to pay for all the
policies. When the children reach a certain age, the parents usually ask

them to take over the policies, and the children, knowing the importance of proper burial, usually do so gladly.

When an islander has moved away and then died, every possible effort is made to return the body to the island for burial among relatives and friends. The desire to be buried at home is also very common among the Igbo, Yoruba, and other Nigerian peoples, who believe without question that the dead are dependent on their ancestors for spiritual nourishment and thus must be buried among them to find peace.[50] By ongoing tradition, Sea Island burial places are densely wooded and are considered to be the sacred abodes of the spirits.

A burial tradition once practiced widely on the Sea Islands and in rural areas of the deep South, though it is now dying out, is the placing of articles such as pottery, spoons, dishes, and other items belonging to the deceased person on the grave, in case the deceased might need or want them in afterlife. Even those scholars hesitant to ascribe other practices observed on the islands to African influences have readily accepted the African basis of this tradition.[51] I have seen the same practices among the Igbo and Ibebio, and it was at one time not unusual in West Africa for boxes of the dead person's possessions—clothes, hardware, and crockery, for example—to be laid by the body, which was not interred but left on top of the ground and covered with branches and leaves.[52]

On the Sea Islands children's graves were traditionally decorated with favorite toys, broken glasses and cups, and money banks always containing a few pennies. The islanders could not explain why the glasses and cups were broken before they were put on a grave. Some said that it was done to decrease the chance of someone's stealing the items; others commented they were merely copying what they had always seen done. The old customs, however, are now being replaced for both children and adults by the use of fancy headstones and cement vaults, which have come to be thought more prestigious signs of one's love for the deceased person.

Sea Island funerals are often very sad and solemn occasions, but they are also very emotional, as are most of the religious services. People attend a funeral to pay their respects to the deceased, but even more to pay their respects to the deceased's family. Each person is given a funeral as elaborate as the family and friends can make it, and the church is packed as full for the funeral of a young child as it would

The Sea Islanders have traditionally buried their dead in densely wooded areas. These areas are considered sacred and are thought to harbor the spirits of the deceased.

be for that of an elderly person who had acquired many friends and relatives over the years.

The Sea Island churches are the mainstay of the community and are always full of life, vigor, and energy. Many of them have long and illustrious histories. The Hebrew United Presbyterian Church on Johns Island, for example, was organized in 1868 after the white Presbyterian church no longer admitted blacks to worship at its services or in its building. The blacks held services in a bush tent until a new building could be put together out of lumber left on Seabrook and Kiawah beaches by a shipwreck. At the time the island could be reached only by boat, and according to the church historian, the organizing members gathered the wood, put it on a raft, and floated it to the construction site.

Brick Church, located on St. Helena Island, is a Baptist church with an even longer history. It was constructed by slaves for their masters in 1855. In 1862 the slaves, who had been permitted to worship in the balcony, took over the church when the white masters fled the island during the Civil War. Before Penn School (the first normal industrial and agricultural school for the education of blacks in South Carolina) was erected in 1864, the school's founder, Laura Towne, held classes in this church. An elegant two-story structure, Brick Church has been standing firm and serene for more than a century on the grounds of what is now Penn School Center.[53]

The Sea Island church services are lively and enthusiastic. At a good Baptist or African Methodist Episcopal (AME) Sunday morning service, the singing and praising will be audible for many miles. If there is a pianist, drummer, guitarist, or tambourinist, the service is even more energetic. The musical instruments are secondary, however, to the congregation's expressions of joy through handclapping, handshaking, and general rocking and swaying. It is literally impossible to attend these services and not be moved to participate actively. Even the smallest child attempts to move in time to the beat of the songs. The rhythm is also a very important part of the sermons. The minister uses many rhetorical devices to involve his congregation in the service, chief of which is the repetition of words and phrases at the beginning and end of each statement (see Chapter 3). The parishioners are mesmerized by the flow, rhythm, and steady recurrence of the repetitions, and their responses keep the service alive and active.

Brick Church on St. Helena Island was constructed by slaves. Some of the first classes for former slaves in South Carolina were held here.

Often the test of a good Sea Island minister is how well he can arouse and excite his parishioners. Most of the ministers are from the area and know well the rhetorical skills and techniques necessary to keep a congregation involved in the service. From the time when young children begin going to the church services, they learn that rhetorical skills are to be praised, practiced, and deeply venerated as essential characteristics of learned people. Learning, to the islanders, does not necessarily mean college education. Most of the Sea Island ministers have had no formal education at all, yet they could equal and surpass the most prolific expositors of the canons of rhetoric. For example, though this speaker has never heard of Cicero or studied the classical theories of rhetoric, note the unusual skill with which he makes his plea to the congregation, creating the long, flowing, masterfully constructed phrases characteristic of Ciceronian style:

> Heavenly Father
> Look at Reverend Pinckney one more time
> Who is going to unfold the word of eternal truth
> Want you to please, dear Jesus
> Give him a silver trumpet
> [So] he can coax and call some more ushers into this fold
> And then, then, then, my Master
> Look at the mistress of ceremonies
> Jesus
> Want you to plant her feet deep down in the soil, Master
> Where she'll never be [up]rooted by the storm of life[54]

Often when a sermon is completed, the minister will begin to sing. It is essential for a Sea Island minister to be a good singer as well as a good speaker. Singing is a regular part of the islanders' daily lives. Many older people sing with fervor and passion as they work in their gardens or in the fields, even when they are alone. Singing is thought to be good for the body, the spirit, and the soul: it enlivens the spirit, which permeates the soul, giving it spiritual strength, and the soul in turn revitalizes the body with physical strength to carry on in times of despair or when physically exhausted. During the church services singing often stirs and excites an already "happy" congregation. When the music begins, some of the congregants throw up their hands, jerking and shaking their bodies in the movements of the shout. The music starts slowly and softly, gradually increasing in tempo while the shouters strive to keep up with it; it becomes louder and faster until they are totally spent.

The call-and-response style is still the tradition of worship in Sea Island churches, just as it is in most southern black churches. The minister calls out a statement, and the congregation repeats it or gives a rhythmic and raucous reply. Though many of the men act as responders to the ministers, few shout or become "happy" as many of the women do. However, those who do join in the movements of the shout do so with considerable zeal. These frenzied shouts are related to the practices of certain African religious cults.[55] In 1904 a woman wrote of her encounters with the spirituals and shouts of the Sea Islands and asked an inhabitant what explained them. The respondent replied that when the preacher read from the Bible how those "dry bones ter lib ergin," something deep within her would come to life and she would begin to holler and sing some old "shout" song from Africa.[56] I observed similar call-and-response services in Nigeria: though I could not always understand what was being said in the language of the service, I found that I could nevertheless join in singing the reply.

Today there are many customs and practices unique to the Sea Islands and to parts of Africa which offer investigators rich insights into African and African-American traditions. The Sea Island language and oral literature did not develop and survive apart from the social and cultural environment which produced them. The extended family household and the Sea Island burial customs, religious beliefs, and styles of worship are no less evidence of African roots and preservations than is the language itself. As long as these roots remain viable, the Sea Island people will maintain their cultural integrity; only when such traditional roots die will their culture die. I hope that an awareness of these influences upon the culture will aid in understanding the African influences upon the language and literature discussed in the following chapters.

# 2

---

# The Folk Literature

Some folk de gift fe lie.

*Some folks are gifted liars (storytellers).*

## Oral Presentation

During the latter part of the nineteenth century and the early part of the twentieth century folklorists like Joel Chandler Harris, Charles C. Jones, Elsie C. Parsons, and Ambrose Gonzales were quite thorough in their collections of tales, myths, legends, and other forms of verbal art in the Gullah-speaking areas of South Carolina and Georgia.[1] Until very recently, little contemporary work had been undertaken on the Sea Islands in folklore and literature. Today studies in oral traditions have grown beyond the tales and the various ways in which their plots can be varied, improved, or altered for the worse to encompass communicative forces peripheral to the tales themselves.[2] The study of oral literature involves more than just the collection and classification of tales. It is expanding to include such things as proxemics and various pragmatic forces inclusive of atmosphere and audience participation which combine to help create a good tale.

As Western cultures are gifted with a long tradition of written literature, the Gullah performers are likewise gifted with techniques and methods of communicative interactions characteristic of a long tradition of African and African-American oral literature. Unlike the writer, who is often left to create his characters in isolation and solitude, and who is at liberty to take a few days, a week, a month, and in many cases years to fill up a page with words carefully selected to create a certain mood and elicit a certain response, the oral performer must be prepared to create and perform his entire tale within a reasonably short period of time.[3] He does not and cannot perform effectively in isolation. He is influenced immediately by the occasion of the tale, and the atmosphere in which and the audience for whom he is performing. His tale is designed not to be read but to be performed and heard. In written transcriptions of oral literature the words are captured on the page, while the real flavor of the tales and the real artistry of the teller—the actual narration, the actual "telling of the tale" by a gifted and skillful performer—are lost.

Because the many communicative techniques used in storytelling, both verbal and nonverbal, are outside the realm of written literature, until fairly recently they were not felt to be important in written interpretations of Sea Island or other oral traditions. Collections by Parsons and others are indeed excellent in the depiction of characteristic features of plot, but they are devoid of the many kinesic communicative techniques that a teller uses to engage his listeners' attention and actually mesmerize them with gestures—hand movements, a turning of the head, a long pause, a shifting of the eyes, a long knowing stare. Yet kinesics are a part of the oral performance, and much that is communicated through gesture has not been accounted for in written transcriptions of Sea Island oral literature. Even obvious verbal techniques like mimicry, repetition, ideophones (words which convey images and meaning through their sound), and rhetorical questions often fail to be taken into consideration, an omission that subtracts substantially from the beauty of the tales even as it obscures cultural methods of communication and expression.[4]

While it is too much to expect one discipline to teach us to be linguists, ethnologists, folklorists, and anthropologists, the common element among these and other disciplines is the commitment to interpreting and understanding the human interaction in language and culture. The need for interdisciplinary approaches to the study of human behavior is becoming increasingly more apparent. David DeCamp, for example, drew attention to this need for exchange of information and ideas between linguists and scholars in related fields as a result of his efforts to scale sequential language data to form what he calls a linguistic continuum. Though he was the first to apply the technique to linguistic data, DeCamp found that as a general procedure it has been known to psychologists and sociologists as the Guttman Scalogram Analysis for over twenty years.[5]

Dell Hymes also asserts that "a certain kind of information slips away" because of the lack of interdisciplinary approaches. To take an example, linguists, folklorists, and anthropologists rely on language samplings primarily for content, which provides an excellent means of delineating and analyzing elements of various cultures. Though folklorists and anthropologists may extract enough linguistic information to specify verbal genres—tales, prayers, myths, orations—they seldom specify features that one must know if one is actually to recognize instances of these genres in performance. On the other hand, linguists abstract grammar, for example, from speech data and tell us which utterances in sequences are grammatical and which are ungrammatical but they tell us little, if anything, about the various styles, modes, or contexts in which a given utterance may occur. Thus, while anthropologists acquire knowledge of social behavior and linguists acquire knowledge of language behavior, valuable information about cultures and language escapes when neither linguists nor anthropologists provide us with what Hymes calls the actual function of language within a society. We cannot assume, he goes on to say, that language has a homogenous function in every community, because ethnographic records suggest, for example, that "talk for talk's sake" is far from universal. Among the Gbaya of Central Africa, no one is regarded as skilled in narration; among the Wishram Chinook of the Columbia River, one does not talk when one has nothing that needs to be said; among the Paliyans of South India, by the age of forty men are reported as seldom speaking at all, and a talkative person is regarded with suspicion.[6]

In the area of nonverbal communication, Ray Birdwhistell discovered that body gestures in context had meaning "astonishingly like words in language." In the English, American, and German kinesic systems that he studied, he discovered that "there are body behaviors which function like significant sounds, that combine into simple or relatively complex units like words, which are combined into much longer stretches of structured behavior like sentences or even paragraphs." Gestures are culturally linked, and no one body position or motion can be said to be universal; no facial expression or body stance will convey the same meaning in every society.[7] Alfred Hayes summarizes Birdwhistell's basic assumptions underlying the systematic study of bodily movement and motions as follows:

1. Like other events in nature, no body movement or expression is without meaning in the context in which it appears.
2. Like other aspects of human behavior, body posture, movement, and facial expression are patterned and thus, subject to systematic analysis.
3. While recognizing the possible limitations imposed by particular biological substrata, until otherwise demonstrated, the systematic body motion of the members of a community is considered a function of the social system to which the group belongs.
4. Visible body activity like audible acoustic activity systematically influences the behavior of other members of any particular group.
5. Until otherwise demonstrated such behavior will be considered to have an investigable communicational function.
6. The meanings derived therefrom are functions both of the behavior and of the operations by which it is investigated.
7. The particular biological system and the special life experience of any individual will contribute idiosyncratic elements to his kinesic system, but the individual or symptomatic quality of these elements can only be assessed following the analysis of the larger system of which his is a part.[8]

Some familiarity with body movements is important to the discussion of Sea Island literature because the performances of the individual are related to the function of the community of which he is a member, and have meaning in that context. Body expressions otherwise unique to certain African ancestral patterns may remain in the Sea Island communities, just as there are parallels in the language itself and in styles of dance and worship.

Included in this discussion are examples of individual performing styles which are variations on a larger system of community-expected and -accepted behavior patterns during a storytelling event. According to Richard Dorson, there is a "group repertoire." There are indeed patterns of movements characteristic of *inland* black storytellers which are directly related to the culture as a whole. It was once assumed that most people in a subculture told the same tales in the same way. There is a very definite repertoire of gestures common to southern black storytellers; every storyteller has command of these particular gestures and every southern black storyteller has these features in common with other members of the group. On closer observation of individual performers, however, we see that there is much variation and individuality of style. Once the group repertoire has been established, we can more clearly see the distinctions among performers.[9]

Beyond the area of kinesics, other nonverbal communicative interactions include such intrinsic components as the setting and atmosphere for storytelling and the degree to which audience participation influences and is actually a part of a Sea Island tale. Lacking these essential elements, most written versions of Sea Island, Caribbean, and some West African literatures appear as short, loosely strung-together episodic tales. The tales alone are barren and incomplete. They do not show the frequent words and phrases interjected by the listeners, nor do they indicate the subtle manner in which the speaker calls on them actually to help him along in telling his tale. Phillip Noss elaborates on this point: "When one reads tales that are meant to be presented orally, usually in a language other than the original, with little awareness of the cultural setting or the aesthetic principles and assumptions underlying the tale, it is not surprising if he concludes that the tales are merely action-packed episodes involving stock characters whose only dimension may be comic."[10]

The Western reader has been conditioned to judge language and literature through preconceived notions of the content of what an author writes, the organization and degree of development, and the style of the writing. The words are not heard, but a good writer's fervent hope is that the impact of the words will be felt, and consequently much of the writer's effort must be devoted to this task. In oral literature the performance, inclusive of audience participation, is as important as and in most cases more important than the actual content of the tale. For not only are the words heard, visualized, and felt, the whole narrative is actually experienced as one experiences a play. The characters that the performer creates are only as vivid and lifelike as the teller is able to make them. And how vivid they are made is often dependent on how enthusiastic the audience is. An excellent performer, when he slaps his hands together and says "Bam! That one stuck!" can make the audience experience the impact of the blow that Ber Rabbit delivers to the tar baby. As the speaker gradually raises his hand higher and higher in the air to indicate the height to which the buzzard takes the monkey from the ground far below (see "The Buzzard and the Monkey" in Chapter 3), the audience shares the imbalance and giddiness that the monkey feels. With varying degrees of animation, the teller can, like the writer, hypnotize his listeners and compel them to suspend any disbelief and fully participate in the events of the tale. But unlike the written word, which can be enjoyed in solitude, whenever and for however long the reader may wish, effective oral presentation is dependent on many factors that are peripheral to the tale itself. The occasion on which a tale is told, the audience to which it is told, and the style and technique of the person doing the telling, among other factors, cannot be ignored in attempting to read written versions of tales which are meant to be presented orally. These external forces are as much a part of oral literature as character development and tightly knit plot are of written literature.

## The Setting

The Sea Island tradition has been to tell tales (called "lies" by the islanders) as a form of entertainment. The advent of bridges and electricity, however, has brought about significant changes in the occasions for telling folktales. On more remote islands storytelling is still a common practice, and it is still fairly easy to get a "telling" started. On the more industrialized islands television, with its talking pictures, has all but eliminated the need for oral literature as a form of entertainment. Yet, given the choice, most children seem to favor human contact with a person who really knows how to perform a tale over being entertained by television.

In Africa and on the Sea Islands folktelling is an informal social event with no set place for telling or listening to tales. Any place where people often congregate to talk, or just to sit and listen, is a good place for a telling to begin. I collected some tales under trees, in open fields, riding in the back of pickup trucks, and while shark fishing. Others I obtained at island stores, around fire sites, at juke joints, in front of fireplaces, on front porches, and down on the creek banks. I heard still others in the comfort and privacy of the tellers' homes. All but the last were places where people congregated and the teller had enough people for an audience response.

On rainy days, which are prevalent on the islands owing to their subtropical location, one can find men, women, and children sitting in kitchens smelling the welcome aroma of "hoppin John and bone" cooking in a pot or just sitting, smoking pipes (men and women smoke pipes on the Sea Islands), and watching the torrential rain beat against the windowpanes. The best stories I collected on the Sea Islands and in Africa, however, were ones I heard at night in front of the fireplaces when all the daily tasks were completed, supper had been served, the children had been bathed, and everyone was relaxed, content, and gazing into the open fire. The fire had a hypnotic effect, and one's imagination could easily see forms amid the light and shadows of the flames while one listened to the teller unravel his tale.

During the cold season on the Sea Islands (*harmattan* in Africa), yams (or *ji,* the Igbo name for a kind of potato) are often covered with the hot coals of the fire, baked, and offered as refreshments to the entertainer, who never seems to fail to make his tale more pleasing as a result. Gin, homemade brews, and other warming drinks are often passed around if there is a good group of tellers and listeners. In Igbo, Yoruba, and Ibebio villages fresh palm wine, chilled or served at room temperature, and cola nuts are always welcome refreshments during storytelling times.

Though everyone is potentially capable of telling a tale, I soon learned that not everyone can tell a *good* tale. Sea Island informants with whom I spent much time over several years often attempted to tell stories only in an effort to help me along with my work. Others felt a strong need to compensate me for coming such a long way to talk to them or to hear their stories. Thus they made efforts to tell tales even when the occasion was not conducive for a telling to begin. In this situation the teller was often tense, rushed, and unprepared to do his best; the tale would often be confused, lacking in plot, and generally uninteresting. But it is well known among the islanders and the Nigerians who the good storytellers are, and after some time I was directed to those tellers well known for their performances of the oral traditions and gifted in the oral technique. In the words of one of the islanders, "some people de gift for lie." The world *lie* has more than one denotation on the Sea Islands: it not only means that one is not telling the truth; it is also a term associated with any kind of fictional tale told primarily for entertainment.

There are certain cultural taboos associated with Sea Island storytelling. More men than women tell tales. Men are expected to be skilled speakers as well as dancers and singers, while women are expected to be responders, doing the clapping and rhetorical backup. Though some women do tell tales, they most often do so in the privacy of their homes when the men are away. Likewise, the Igbo, Yoruba, and Ibebio women seldom tell tales in the company of men, although alone, or in the company of other women and children, some of the Sea Island and African women are avid storytellers.

On occasions when a storytelling contest was held at the community store during my stays on the islands, many women came to hear the stories, though few of them actually told tales themselves. Miss Myma, the elderly Sea Island lady with whom I resided and who accompanied me to most preplanned telling sessions, always told the first tale, but more in an effort to sanction and add approval to the occasion than as a traditional practice. Several women with whom I had spent time over a seven-year period came to the storytelling contest but bluntly refused to tell any stories. After the session ended and the men were awarded the prizes by the island judges, these women approached me and asked that I come by their homes the following day. I did so and was told many tales, as well as given many folk remedies, cures, and songs. One lady, highly respected in the community, permitted me to hold two storytelling contests at her home. However, she refused to come outside to listen to the tales because the audience was comprised primarily of men. I learned that women are not expected to participate in activities that are considered primarily male-oriented activities. Within the Sea Islands as well as within certain African communities, only women who are elderly or held in fairly high social esteem can participate in such activities without fear of censure.

Most of the tales told by women and elderly men are told during the daylight hours just after lunch when they take a break from the daily chores just to "catch some breeze" or "sit in the cool." One elderly gentleman, nearly one hundred years old now, often entertained me for hours with tales, historical events, and reminiscences before he resumed his afternoon plowing with his favorite mule. This man is particularly interesting because he firmly believes that a man should live apart from his wife and family. Until his wife's death very recently, she lived in a fairly large, modern dwelling with her children, grandchildren, and great-grandchildren while he lived in his shanty located behind the main house and near the other homes within his yard area. His wife prepared his meals and brought them to him at mealtimes and then returned to her own home. Since her death, his granddaughter has continued the practice.

Another elderly friend and informant often sat in the hallway of his shanty, with the front and back doors open to let the breeze flow through the house, and told of Ber Rabbit and times past in vivid detail. Sometimes it seemed that Ber Rabbit was indeed a real character to him, one he had actually encountered and greeted on his many journeys down Sea Island paths.

The Sea Island children are aware of the "old-time stories" such as those about Ber Rabbit and his many companions, but most under the age of twelve told me stories that they had learned in school, and not those characteristic of the Sea Island tradition. Television and improved educational facilities account in part for this change. However, the skill in telling and the ability to retain the old-time stories appear to be related to the degree of modernization of the island. On the more remote islands, including Wadmalaw and Daufuski, many children are avid and skillful storytellers in the old tradition.

Nonetheless, few Sea Island children between the ages of eight and twelve can match the skill and intricate detail in description that the Igbo, Yoruba, and Ibebio children display in captivating an audience and unraveling a tale. Though color television is a common sight in Nigerian cities like Lagos, Aba, Owerri, Calabar, and Eket, the village children are far less likely to have access to television or radio. As would be expected, these children are far more expert in the art of telling a story than even Nigerian city children, probably because village children are still gathered and told stories frequently as a form of entertainment.

Anytime was a good time for the African children to tell stories. But, as on the Sea Islands, the best stories were told in the late evening around the fire sites when a good group had come together to relax and be entertained after the activities of the day were ended.

## The Audience

Today, as noted earlier, the extended family is still a practiced tradition on the Sea Islands. The inhabitants, like their West African forebears, seem to be communal people. They live in close proximity to their families and neighbors and appear to enjoy companionship and group cooperation more than solitude and isolation. This social sharing and seeming congeniality is as vivid in their literature as it is in their daily lives. An overt expression of group participation is witnessed in the interplay between speaker and audience in folktales, speeches, and sermons. In Sea Island public speaking, the audience is as important for a good performance as the performer himself. As in Africa, the best audience is a lively audience: one in which the listeners participate actively in the narration by responding to certain cues from the performer. In really exciting performances speaker and audience become so intermeshed and such oneness is achieved that it may appear that the response is an actual part of the tale itself. This is particularly true, of course, for tales well known to both audience and performer.

Unless tales are told in the privacy of a home with very few listeners, the speaker will rarely begin a performance without some "warming up." Among the Igbo and Ibebio, for example, formal folktales are preceded by songs and selected tales called (in Igbo) *akuko eji awake nti,* which means the first tale told to awaken or to enlighten the ear so that it absorbs the real meaning of what follows. Among the Igbo, before any tale begins, the speaker greets his listeners by saying "Chakpii [Are you ready?]." And the listeners respond, "Haa [We are ready to welcome your story!]." (These words are repeated at the end of each story, where they may be read as, respectively, "My story has ended" and "Thank you, storyteller, for your tale.") While the islanders do not seem to have any tale prescribed for the sole purpose of opening telling sessions, they do have some patterns for preparing to tell informal folktales.

The timing and atmosphere are very important to telling, hearing, and collecting good tales. If the audience is not properly prepared, the occasion is not conducive to good tales. The atmosphere must be relaxed; the teller not only must be willing to tell a tale but must have an audience and sufficient time to tell the story. The more listeners, the better the tales seem to be. In large groups, even when a storytelling event has been planned, it often takes quite a while for a session to begin. The pattern seems to be that everyone in the group will at first pretend not to know any stories, or even how to tell one. If it is known that one of the people in the group is a good performer, then someone may point him out and ask him to tell a tale. He of course refuses.

Miss Josephine is an avid storyteller. She, like most Sea Island women, continues to wear a headwrap.

Then members of the group may sit and tease each other for a while, telling jokes, playing the dozens, taking a little nip, or just sitting and enjoying one another's company. When I was there, after the group had kidded around until everyone was laughing and in a fairly congenial mood, I was usually granted permission to turn the recorder on, and it was time to tell some tales.

With older storytellers, the sessions often begin with a song, religious or otherwise. During the singing, the members of the group join in enthusiastically, singing, clapping their hands, or swaying with the rhythm. After the song ends, the audience is usually ready to hear a good tale. Regardless of the ages of the members of the group, the most impressive stories are always told after the group has had a chance to talk, kid around, play the dozens, sing, or just be "sporty." The friendly teasing and cordial verbal exchange relaxes the audience and serves the same purpose as the *akuko eji awake nti* in Igbo: it prepares the listeners so that they will participate in the telling of the tales by responding to certain cues given by the performers.

A speaker may begin his tale by indicating that he is going to tell a story about Ber Rabbit. The audience (or a given respondent) may clap their hands, laugh, and rock back and forth to indicate their interest and repeat, "Ber Rabbit, Ber Rabbit, Ber Rabbit!" This response demonstrates that the speaker has engaged their interest and attention and that they are now prepared to hear his tale. As the tale progresses, if the teller is entertaining and effective, the listeners will continue to respond to his every word, laughing and joking, clapping their hands, and urging him on with his tale. The audience is not a captive one; if the teller is not skilled in narrative technique, and his tale or delivery is uninteresting, then the listeners may wander away to get something to drink or talk to others and return only when a better speaker is talking. This response undoubtedly has an effect on the teller, who may try to hurry and finish his story so that someone else can have a turn.

Most audiences react to onomatopoeic words, repetitions, and chants. They respond as a chorus by repeating some of the speaker's words or phrases in unison or singularly. A practice very common both in Africa and on the Sea Islands is an interplay between the speaker and a given member of the audience. In an Igbo village, for example, Raphael Amaugo often called on his friend Cornelius Onunwa to help him remember the details of a story that Raphael knew quite well. The call for assistance is a device to keep the audience abreast of the details by pretending that some part of the tale has been temporarily forgotten. Often the member of the audience called upon will reply, "That's the way it happened" or "You are telling it right!" Even if the speaker is not telling a story in just the way a member of the audience remembers it, seldom will anyone openly dispute the manner in which the tale is told. This is apparently an unwritten rule of courtesy of both Igbo and Gullah cultures.

In addition to pretending to forget, a speaker may turn to a particular respondent, call him by name, and ask, for example, "You know what I mean, don't you, Doc?" The Sea Island respondent may then answer, "Ki! I know what you mean, man!" This is a reassuring device for both speaker and audience because the other members as well will usually answer, "I know what you mean! I know what you mean!" Likewise, in the narration of a historical event, members of the audience who are familiar with the event may inject a word of understanding or support by adding a personal comment, such as "I remember . . . I remember the place." The audience may encourage the speaker by calling out, "Tell the story . . . tell the story!"

Another practice characteristic of Gullah and Igbo, Yoruba, and Ibebio speakers in particular is that of telling a tale seemingly for one individual. A speaker may single out a person whom he knows, or one whom he may not know well, and seem to speak directly to this person, ignoring all others. He has eye contact with this one hearer alone and may even turn his back to other members of the audience sitting next to him. This turning of the back is fairly common in some West African communities and is apparently not a discourteous practice; I have never seen it offend any member of the groups observed. In fact, two informants on the Sea Islands who are close friends and avid storytellers often turn their backs to each other or sit sideways so that they are neither facing nor sitting directly next to each other. When they tell tales, each one acts as a respondent for the other, yet they turn around only when some point to be stressed requires the use of the hands as a visual aid. In most Western cultures, turning one's back to another person is an overt sign of disregard or disrespect. In Sea Island communities, however, one can observe this behavior in churches or other gathering places. Two men will often sit on each end of a church bench in such a manner that their backs are turned slightly away from each other. During the entire course of a sermon, they will turn around only to nod agreement to each other, to say, "Amen," or just to recognize each other's presence before resuming their former positions. This behavior is observed more often in men than in women or children, though I have seen it in young boys during the course of a storytelling event in Nigeria and on the Sea Islands.

The expectation of audience participation among Sea Island and Nigerian audiences contrasts rather sharply with the behavioral expectations of most Western audiences, who sit in silence, not necessarily because they do not enjoy the message of the speaker but because silence is a cultural sign of respect and courtesy. It is not known whether responding is characteristic of all African or related cultures, but Ruth Finnegan relates an identical practice, "replying," used by the Limba speakers of northern Sierra Leone: the audience assists the speaker by answering, "Me!" According to Finnegan, replying

> also refers to the actions of the listeners when someone is making a formal speech; they should not interrupt the flow of his presentation but should "reply" to his argument, perhaps by echoing his words or answering his rhetorical questions, perhaps by only a grunt or murmur at suitable intervals; in this way they are thought to play the important part of supporting or noting his main points as they are made. "Replying" in song is also an important practice, applied in particular to the way in which the women as a group reply in chorus to the song of a soloist, and in this way take an essential part in the whole activity.[11]

The practice of listener response in communicative events not only is common in storytelling, sermons, and speeches but is a vivid part of daily social interaction in Igbo, Ibebio, Yoruba, and Sea Island communities. The act of responding is a method of showing approval and understanding—or disapproval or misunderstanding.

For a speaker's listeners to be verbally responsive to his cues during the time he is speaking is a very good indication that they agree with or understand what he says. If they sit quietly and do not respond verbally during the course of the speaking event, then the speaker can be assured that they have either not enjoyed his presentation or not understood what has been said. Thus understanding the importance of audience participation and response in such communities helps in the understanding of their language and literature in its social context.

It is to be hoped that more objective methods of describing communicative behavior in oral traditions will be included in future written versions of oral literature.

## The Storytellers

The performance of an individual within a culture is directly related to the expectations of the culture, and the individual performer usually respects these expectations. The Sea Island storytellers follow techniques for telling stories that have been passed on as tradition. The best storytellers are those who know how to evoke lifelike images in a listener's mind and create suspense and drama through the interactions of characters. How these goals are achieved is determined by the individual storyteller. The most common devices used to create intensity and excitement include repetition of words and phrases at strategic points in a story; mimicry, which may involve anything from the shrieking sounds of a hog or the loping motions of a running wolf to the twittering sound of a partridge as he inadvertently moves through an oat field; voice modulation, ranging from a very high-pitched, shrill tone indicative of nervousness, agitation, and excitement to a very low-pitched, quiet tone suggesting cautiousness and reserve; and various bodily gestures, such as placing the left hand in the right armpit and pumping the right arm up and down against the body to produce the sound of a large animal galloping in the distance.

Oral style, like written style, is idiosyncratic. The individual speaker will embroider his own style on certain features and thus add uniqueness to his performance. The tellers vary. Some are very fluent and the words flow with ease. Some hesitate and search for words and often resort to *ah, wime,* or other fillers to try to unify what they are saying. Some tellers are better at certain kinds of narratives than others. I found that Mr. Henry would not tell any tales about Ber Rabbit and his uncanny ways, but he could talk for hours about historical events such as the Garvey movement or the 1893 storm. His style, like his topics, was always elevated and serious. On the other hand, Mr. Oree would tell only humorous tales, and his preference for trivial topics was reflected in his playful, jesting performances. Personality, however, is not necessarily woven into an individual's personal delivery style, because extremely reserved and nontalkative people may tell tales which are lengthy, raucous, and sometimes even bawdy. The ways in which various narratives can be treated and presented are best illustrated by discussing some individual storytellers, their personal histories, the types of stories they tell, and their method of presentation. From this information the reader may more fully appreciate the range of styles falling within the Sea Island tradition.

*Mr. Ted Williams,* in his late forties, is a family man and one of few blacks to own a substantial amount of land on Wadmalaw Island. Along with farming that land, he owns and runs a local grocery store. As a young man he left the island to try city work, "but I didn't stay. I always think about home. I always want to come back home. And I always wanted to work for myself."[12] Mr. Ted is an influential deacon in his church, and in this capacity he participates widely in fund-raising drives and other community activities. He is a very sociable person; he likes being around people and is a welcome visitor to any home. As a deacon he is a weekly speaker before the church congregation and knows well how to inspire and excite people. His seemingly natural public speaking skills are easily carried over to his skill and ability in telling a good tale. Mr. Ted has no preference for types of folk narratives; his repertoire ranges from the humorous exploits of a scheming buzzard to serious oratory on the design of the universe. He is known best not for a particular subject but simply for his ability to tell a story, a "good lie." I found his personal style probably the most effective of all in eliciting audience participation. Once he began a tale, he was an enthusiastic teller. He amused his listeners by walking around, joking, laughing, and inspiring everyone to become involved with his story. Because he seemed to enjoy performing, any tale he told was welcomed by his listeners. He was playful and constantly teased the audience by saying that this was his last tale, and he would not tell another one. Likewise, he was a catalyst to other tellers, who often tried to imitate his style and vied with him in trying to tell the best tale. Few matched his technique, though some told more intricate stories.

Mr. Ted usually stood when he began a tale and seldom sat down until it was finished. When he did sit, it was only for a moment, and even then some part of his body was in constant motion. His hands

A leading member of the community on Wadmalaw Island, Mr. Ted Williams is known for his ability to tell a good story.

were often spread to emphasize a point, or his leg would swing back and forth like a pendulum to suggest the passage of time. When not emphasizing a point, he often rotated his hand at the wrist as if keeping silent time with the rhythm of the tale. Facial expressions and voice modulations were an important part of his personal delivery. For example, many informants told the tale "Ber Rabbit and the Tar Baby." However, when Ber Rabbit begged the man not to throw him in the briar patch, Mr. Ted gave meaning to the word *beg*. His voice became whiny and whimpering, and his face took on the appearance of one in great distress. He squinched his eyes, wrinkled his nose, and in a high-pitched voice said, "Ple-e-e-ase don't throw me in there." On the page these words are almost lifeless, but when he uttered them in conjunction with such movements as making faces, raising his arms to his chest, crooking his hands and fingers, and trembling as if in mortal terror, the listeners went wild with laughter. What he said in his tales seemed almost irrevelant when compared to the many movements, expressions, and exaggerations that he used in actually performing a given tale.

Most of Mr. Ted's tales ended with a moral; if one was not readily apparent, he made one up. He liked to do what he considered moralizing and philosophizing about life. The language of his tales was contemporary Gullah, with such features as the preverbal markers *de, ben, bina,* and *don;* lack of inflections like *-ed* and *-ing;* and little of the subject-verb concord that one expects in standard English. These features, which among others distinguished his speech as contemporary Gullah and not black English or standard English (see Chapter 4), were part of what made his tales so appealing to other Gullah speakers. If he had approximated a form of standard English, as he sometimes did (see "Peter and the Rock," for instance—the switch is very obvious) he would not have been telling the tale in the language and style of the Gullah-speaking community.

*Mr. James Oree* is quite the opposite of Mr. Ted. He is approximately thirty-six years old. He seldom attends church; he drinks in excess; and he loves to be among the sweet ladies of the community who "like for have good time!" He enjoys his life immensely. He claims to have worked hard when he was able to work. Recently, however, he has been in failing health, and work has not "agreed" with him. Those who know him like him well. He is generally a very talkative person, once he decides that he wants to "waste" his time with you. During the period that I spent on the Sea Islands, he was always helpful but agreed to tell stories to me only at the request of the lady next door, whose encouraging words were, "You know some old-time story, so tell she some!" And some very excellent ones he told! He was quite the comedian, and all of his tales were humorous and lively (see "Ber Rabbit, Ber Wolf, and the Butter"). Even when he attempted a serious tale, it seemed to come out funny.

Like Mr. Ted, however, he had a unique personal delivery which captivated his audience and caused them to respond well to his style of expression. For example, he always took his time to tell a story, and the leisure and sheer idleness with which he spoke were part of his uniqueness as a good storyteller. As is characteristic of most Sea Island tales, his stories were series of action-packed episodes. Yet he never stood up, walked around, or moved unless he felt compelled to do so to emphasize some point. In fact, during most of his telling time, he sat with his eyes half closed, as if contemplating the character's next move. At times he seemed to be unaware of an audience; he seemed instead to be carrying on a dialogue as though he were one of the characters himself. For example, instead of introducing direct speech with the formulaic verb *say,* Mr. Oree often pretended to be the characters and simply spoke their dialogue. His ability to modulate his very deep bass voice to take on the character and speaking habits of various participants in a story seemed to be one of his most artistic techniques, adding life, zest, and interest to his tales. But even more effective was the deliberate casualness of his style, which kept the listeners hanging on every word.

There was very little actual description in Mr. Oree's tales—he used very few words, in fact, and thus even fewer long sentences. Yet the listeners were seemingly able to intuit the details of his story from the description that he did give and the slow, contemplative manner in which he told the tale. He used more ideophones than many of the other tellers, and he was also extremely adept at producing certain sounds. For example, this is the way Mr. Oree represented the caution in Ber Rabbit's steps as he tries to manuever past a hunter with a gun in an open oat field:

Rabbit jump. . . . [He closed his eyes and contemplated, swaying back and forth as if counting to himself.] Rabbit jump. . . .

[Again he swayed back and forth as if counting to himself.] De dup . . . de dup . . . de dup, going in [a pause], going in that wood, you know. Bi-i-i-g oat field."

Likewise, he imitated the chittering sound of the partridge as he inadvertently follows Ber Rabbit into the open oat field:

Partridge . . . Ha! . . . [He paused as if contemplating the partridge's character.] He *crazy,* you know! . . . He ain't know that Ber Rabbit done got him! He gone. . . . He gone out there. He kickeri, kickeri. [Suddenly he opened his eyes and slapped his hands together.]
Bam!
Dead!

At this point in the speaker's narrative, his listeners had become rather involved with the suspense of his tale. It is unlikely that he would have been more effective if he had been more prolix or more descriptive. He elicited a gasp of amazement from his listeners merely by slapping his hands together to imitate the blast from the gun (*Bam!*) and by conveying the partridge's swift and instant death in the simple word *Dead!*

The absence of very much description in Mr. Oree's accounts is typical of Sea Island tales. The language that is used, however, suggests to the mind far more detail than could ever be set down. For example, the mention of a big oat field evokes colors (shades of browns, beiges, and greens) and a sense of vastness and openness. By choosing not to describe every detail of a scene, the narrators permit the listeners to create in their own minds certain images and impressions which give the tale added dimension. This, then, may account in part for the usual description of Sea Island literature, in written transcription, as short, incomplete, and lacking in the characteristics of sustained literary work. These standards, of course, are standards by which Western cultures have traditionally judged written literature, and they just do not apply to the literature of a people whose tradition has always been oral.

Again, as I noted, gestures were not an inherent part of Mr. Oree's style; rather, it was his whole body posture—sitting, half reclining, eyes half closed, his feet apart, his arms and hands turned slightly inward and resting on his lap—which seemed to communicate to his audience. But just as, according to Birdwhistell, all body movement or expression has meaning, so does the absence of movement. Though Mr. Oree held himself nearly still, making gestures only to emphasize a point in an episode, he held his audience captive through story after story.

The language Mr. Oree used is characteristic of contemporary Gullah speech on Wadmalaw Island. He did not get formal education beyond the tenth grade, and he has no desire for social prestige on the island. Thus he has felt little if any need to adapt his speech to conform to that of the more affluent, better-educated, rising social class. In his tales one finds the influence of outside social forces in some of the words used, but much of the content, structure, and language of the tales remain unquestionably Gullah, and most probably African in origin.

*Mr. Henry Gibbs,* one of the oldest members of his community, is now approximately one hundred. Until recent years he was always an active member of his church. He is a fairly well-educated man, reads and writes very well, can see well enough to plow a garden each year with his favorite mule, but can hear only when he takes a "notion" to do so. He is always serious and majestic in manner and appearance. Likewise, his oratory is always on matters he feels to be grave, profound, historical, and factual. He will tolerate no discussions of trivia. He told me that he participated in the Marcus Garvey movement and that he can remember his parents talking about "slavery and the 'buckra' [white man] as good as yesterday." He claims to know every family on Wadmalaw Island and most of those on adjoining islands. He is held in grand esteem and awe by his family, friends, and neighbors. Mr. Henry's life-style is somewhat unusual: he keeps all of his belongings in his shanty, located centrally to his wife's home and to his children's and grandchildren's homes. He prefers the solitude of his own house, he says, so that he can think and reflect without being disturbed by noises from his family. His choice is reminiscent of the separate living quarters characteristic in traditional Igbo, Yoruba, and other West African cultures.

Mr. Henry's narrative style is more descriptive than some Sea Islanders', but this distinction is perhaps related to the subject matter of his narratives, primarily legends and historical accounts, the nature of which requires a certain seriousness in presentation. This personal style does, however, represent a method of expression characteristic of many Sea Island folk narrators, which is anything but comic.

During my stay, most of Mr. Henry's tales were told on his front porch, with people gathered around him. One unusual feature of his delivery was that, even at one hundred years old, he always stood when he was ready to begin a narrative, though unlike Mr. Ted, Mr. Henry seldom walked around as he talked. Amid his listeners, he stood erect and composed in one spot during the whole course of his narrative, which could go on for hours. Many times his wife (now deceased) came and asked him to eat lunch or dinner, or just to let the visitors go home; in the latter case he continued speaking as he followed us to the car.

Sometimes during a long narrative he would stop, take out his handkerchief, wipe his face, and seem to stare out across the open field in front of his home. At these times it was quite obvious that his narrative had brought to his mind memories of times gone past. His eyes, which he himself said would not see much that they had not seen before, became moist. But it was incommensurate with his manner to lose his dignity and composure. Thus, grasping his cane more firmly, he stood quiet, firm and serene, until the moment passed and he was ready to continue his narrative.

Like Mr. Oree, Mr. Henry seemed to command attention through his bodily presence. But in contrast to the casual style characteristic of Mr. Oree, Mr. Henry captivated his audience with seriousness. With his feet planted firmly on the floor, arms held at his side, he made few gestures. To stress a point, he would perhaps raise one arm and point with his entire hand, as opposed to one finger. The other arm generally remained immobile at his side, with the hand slightly opening and closing in a half fist. Little else moved. His face was expressive, but for the most part he told his narratives, one after the other, standing in the same spot.

His voice was strong and clear in spite of his age. While he spoke, silence pervaded the audience. Even children felt the need to whisper a complaint in his presence. His age was certainly a factor, in that the islanders have much respect for the elderly in their communities, especially a member as exalted as Mr. Henry. Nevertheless, his age was not the primary ingredient in his success as an oral artist. His descriptions were very detailed. He made exceptional use of pauses, seemingly in order to permit the listeners to reflect on the content of his narrative; whatever his reason, it was a highly effective technique. During his long pauses, older members often offered a word of encouragement, such as "Tell em, Henry." Mr. Henry would reply, "Shore [sure]! I remember that good as yesterday!"

Like most good Sea Island narrators, Mr. Henry used a highly emotional oratorical method that tended to stimulate and excite his listeners. He frequently used repetition and parallel constructions, with mesmerizing effects. For example, he often spoke of the days of his youth, a time when he lived and worked on a plantation. The simple words "We ben living over there . . . on the white people place . . . the white people place" alone on the page can never capture the emotion of his phrasing or show his grave expression as he paused to reflect. The words had apparently brought to mind untold memories, so many that he felt compelled to repeat the phrase again softly and more deliberately, as if each word had history in itself.

In addition to his various uses of repetition, Mr. Henry would often actually shout out with passionate anger, joy, or excitement. To his exclamations, older members would respond with equal fervor. He would call out the name of a responding member and ask, for example:

"Myma, you ain't know what I bina talk about, do you?"

The respondent (Myma in this case) would reply:

"Yeah man! Shore I bina know!"
"Huh?"
"Yeah! Yeah!"
"But this one here [pointing to a younger member] ain't de know. E [he] ain't even ben born yet."

Appropriately to his topics, Mr. Henry's language had formal overtones even in casual utterances. Thus he retained the elements characteristic of a creolized Gullah speech: one pronoun for both masculine and feminine subjects, a range of preverbal markers, few if any morphological inflections, the introductory or formulaic verb *say,* and other features of the creole tradition (see Chapter 4).

*Miss Deeley* would not reveal her age, nor would she consent to being recorded or permit me to use her last name, but she is one of the most prolific women storytellers that I encountered. She is fifty or more years of age, gets around well, is the oldest member of her household, and is primarily responsible for the total care of more than ten children, ranging in ages from two to sixteen years of age. Some of them are her own children; others are her grandchildren and great-grandchildren. Six of them live with her, and four are left in her care during the day while their parents are away working. I had the pleasure of spending more than two weeks residing with Miss Deeley and her large family. I shared a large room with three of the girls and came to appreciate the effort that went into keeping that room clean and orderly at all times. No one was allowed to retire for the evening without a bath regardless of circumstances. Most of the time, a fire was built around a large black pot in the early evening to heat the water for baths before supper was served. All the children were lined up and given baths in a number-three washtub, given their nightclothes, and served supper around a large handmade wooden table. Miss Deeley had not accepted electricity for her home, so a kerosene lamp was the primary source of light after nightfall. Mealtime was always a pleasure at this home. The last meal of the day often consisted of cowpeas and rice cooked and seasoned with "bone," or rice served with shrimp and other fish caught by the children during the day. There was always hot corn bread and molasses and a bucket of iced tea.

After meals were served, the children gathered around the open fireplace, and Miss Deeley entertained all of us for hours until the fire died down and the sleeping children had to be carried to their beds. This woman was an avid storyteller. Her general procedure was first to get everyone settled. Then she herself could get comfortable in the place always reserved for her by the window. After poking around in the fire until she was satisfied that it was burning well, she would lean back in her chair, take a couple of good bites of tobacco, kept in her apron pocket, and then lift up the youngest child into her lap and begin to reminisce about happenings during the day. She had the ability to tell a range of stories, but she seemed particularly adept at hag, ghost, or other psychological thrillers. She traveled around much in her day as a migrant worker in Arizona and Colorado; she said she heard some of her stories around the campfires there. Others she had learned from her parents and grandparents, and still others she said she had just made up to keep the children entertained.

Miss Deeley was fairly strict with the children. Once she permitted two of the oldest to go to the island store for some "sweet"; she spat some tobacco juice on the ground and told them that they had better be back home before the juice dried. She seemed to delight in playing with the children, however. One evening she told a series of tales about "raw head and bloody bone" and then retired to her room, leaving the children and me sitting, gazing into the fire. Shortly afterward she appeared in the open doorway, down on all fours with a sheet covering her body, her arm and hand outstretched as if she were reaching for one of the children. Everyone, including me, jumped up and ran to the back door calling her name. She then unveiled herself, overjoyed that she had frightened the children but delirious with laughter that she had actually frightened me.

Miss Deeley's telling style differed from most of the men's in that she usually kept her voice low and rather sedate, as did most of the other women who told stories. She did not tell many tales in the animal tradition of trickster. As noted, her favorite topics were "hants," hags, and unusual murders (see "The Three Pear[s], or the Singing Bones"). Her subject matter may have been inspired by the proximity of a grave-yard to her home; her belief that she had seen spirits of people buried there perhaps added realism to her tales both in her mind and in her listeners' minds. She was not a master of facial gestures as Mr. Ted was, but rather captivated her listeners through vocal expressions and voice modulation. Characteristic of her speaking style were low mournful moans, of varying durations and intensities, and subtle ex-clamations at strategic intervals. The low intensity and monotony of her voice contributed significantly to her ability to create suspense through an aura of intense dread and to communicate fear and even terror to her listeners.

The nature of her topics made Miss Deeley's audience a somewhat captive group, and she knew well how to keep them that way. She had a mastery of narrative devices used to test her audience to see if they were indeed abreast of her tale. For example, during a very intense part of a tale, she would often stop, spit tobacco into the fire, and ask one of the children if she had remembered to bring the clothes in off the line, knowing full well that the chore had been done. The child would quickly answer yes and beg her to go on and tell what happened. Satis-fied that she held her listeners' total attention, she continued with her narrative. Given the nature of her topics, her audience communicated with her on a nonverbal level; rarely would anyone dare to make a sound. She seemed to enjoy the spellbinding effect of her narratives not only on the children but on the adults who often came to visit her as well. Many times the children sat with their eyes glued to her face or staring dazed into the fire, hypnotized by the slow, steady rhythm of her voice unfolding the bizarre events of her tale. At times, her voice became so low, and she paused so long, that some of the younger children stirred, and the older ones lashed out in anger at them for disturbing the chilling mood that had been created. In tales of hags, ghosts, and other strange happenings, the audience did not usually respond quickly as they did with other, less suspenseful, tales, primarily because topics such as these were not taken lightly by the islanders. Many are staunch believers in hags, ghosts, voodoo, and the occult. Thus tales of this kind were told not only for entertainment but to inform or to reaffirm the listeners' belief in the existence of these seen and unseen forces rampant throughout the islands and the universe.

Furthermore, such grave topics often had an aesthetic appeal somewhat different from that of funny or historical tales. The audience was not lively, loud, or as energetic as it would be when listening to the exploits of Ber Rabbit. Witty stories are deserving of spirited and excited responses. In listening to tales of the supernatural, the audience tended to be not only quiet but filled with awe and reverence, even more for one who knew of such things by firsthand experience than for the topic itself. There was some verbal interplay between Miss Deeley and her audience, but it was much more subdued than even in prayers and sermons. In prayers and sermons the audience is expected to participate openly in the event. People are free to speak as loud and become as verbally unrestrained as they want "when the spirit hits them." In listening to tales like Miss Deeley's, the audience was restrained both by the subject and by the speaker's use of a lowered, even whispered, tone to help create an eerie effect; many times the listeners had to strain to hear every word. As a result, most displays from the audience were in the form of low moans ("ummmm . . . uh") or an occasional "yeah, man," "shonuf so" or "where you de say you see em?" In these narratives—especially where a story was felt to have an actual basis in fact—the listeners' questions were not rhetorical, and the speaker took time out from the events of the tale to answer them.

Miss Deeley was one of the few informants who still included songs in some of the tales told. Songs are an inherent part of most West African stories, and of stories told throughout the Caribbean, because they give the audience an opportunity to become an active participant in the telling event. Some Sea Island informants who knew many kinds of tales often included songs and thus encouraged the audience to participate in singing the chorus. Many of those who did not know the words to the chorus participated by clapping their hands, patting their feet, or humming along with those who were singing. The Sea Island tales with songs were far more exciting in eliciting a wide response from the audience than those without songs.

Though Miss Deeley is most noted for telling tales of bizarre happenings and supernatural events, I found that the children who were left in her care seemed to remember the words and melodies to the songs in the tales much better than they remembered the unusual events (see "The Three Pear[s]"). This woman's vast repertoire of tales, like her knowledge about various medicinal cures, is perhaps a result of her having given birth to thirteen children, twelve of whom are living. She told me that telling them stories helped keep them occupied and out of trouble. In addition, some of the older children used the same tales and techniques to keep the younger ones amused. Now that most of her own children are grown, she continues the storytelling tradition with the grandchildren and great-grandchildren left in her care. Furthermore, while she does indeed believe in modern medicine, she says she finds that most of the ailments that she and her family have suffered could be cured or helped by various roots that she found on the islands. The most popular of these is the bloodroot, which when boiled makes a reddish tea and is exceptionally good for high blood pressure. The snakcroot, which must be boiled and permitted to stand or age with good whiskey, is very useful for increasing the appetite and eliminating constipation.

Though Miss Deeley would not consent to being recorded, she was patient enough to permit me to take down one story ("The Three Pear[s]") verbatim. This tale represents her language well.

*Mr. Jonas Mickell* became a close friend over a period of years, and I am indebted much to him and his wife for the time and effort they took to help contribute to this and other studies. Mr. Mickell is a well-respected man in his community. He traveled much around the islands by boat in his day and thus always had stories to tell of his adventures. He is sixty or more years old and says that he was somewhat "sporty" with the ladies before he was married, some forty years ago, to his present wife. He admits to directing appreciating glances at a fine-looking woman even today, but says that a look is the extent of his appreciation.

Mr. Mickell attended elementary school on Johns Island, but because he had to work to help support his family, he was forced to quit school during the elementary grades. Yet he has done well for himself. He was in the navy and has worked on various jobs from handyman to longshoreman. He now lives a rather tranquil but satisfying life, with a degree of comfort slightly more sumptuous than that of many islanders.

Mr. Mickell is a gifted storyteller. Many of the tales I heard him tell have direct parallels with some told in Nigeria (see "Ber Rabbit and the Lord"). His speaking style is as characteristic of Sea Island speech as the other informants'. He speaks very rapidly with a very high pitch and tone. In fact, I sometimes found it extremely difficult to understand him when he became engrossed in a narrative. The problem with interpretation was not with his vocabulary, though he knew many old words with African origins; the problem was primarily a phonological one. The rhythm, tempo, and stress with which he pronounced the English words is really one of the most outstanding characteristics of contemporary Gullah speech. Though I had difficulty adjusting to his delivery, the audience composed of speakers born and raised on the Sea Islands had no problem at all, as would be expected.

I found Mr. Mickell's most distinguishing feature to be his use of gestures and repetition. A rapid rate of speaking, sustained high pitch, and strong rhythm are characteristic of the community. Mr. Mickell, however, spoke more quickly than others. The rapid speaking style was enough in itself to create excitement, but the method by which Mr. Mickell used repetition, whether in words or phrases or in parallel structure, helped to intensify the excitement in his rapid series of action-packed episodes. In one tale, for example, he described how a king snake is able to kill other snakes. He conveyed the striking manner in which the king snake coils itself around its victim through a series of words repeated rapidly in succession, "Wrap up, wrap up, wrap up." To illustrate this action, he made his hands into fists and rolled them rapidly over and over in front of him, completing the coiling gesture with a "pssssup" to indicate that the victim is completely immobile within the coils. To show how the king snake stretches its victim and shatters its spinal cord in one quick motion, Mr. Mickell slowly pulled his fist apart to suggest a slow stretching process, saying, "Stretch out, stretch out, stretch out." Then, in a sweeping motion, he tightened his fist and with one violent jerk emphasized the king snake's ultimate quick, spasmodic motion.

Mr. Mickell is a great talker. The speech samples I obtained from him ranged from childhood experiences to tales of the bizarre. He is a good singer and participates in the shouts with enthusiasm. But the outstanding feature in his repertoire is a collection of dozens and dozens of riddles. Riddling is a pastime activity common among the older Sea Island men and women. In fact, Mr. Mickell and one of his close friends often sat for hours telling riddles until one or the other ran out of riddles to tell.

Without a doubt, *Aneatha Brisbane, Miss Myma,* is my closest link to the Sea Island communities. She was born in a shanty, still standing on Wadmalaw Island, and never really ventured far from the site on which it now stands. Her mother lived in the shanty before Miss Myma was born, and when she died, Miss Myma continued to live there until she purchased a one-bedroom trailer some fifteen or twenty years ago. The trailer was a weather-beaten shell of a home consisting of a living room, a kitchen, and a bedroom. It had no running water, no electricity, and no toilet, though it was equipped with appropriate connections. I soon understood that while these things are primary for survival for most Americans, to stay on the Sea Islands I had to be ready to live without them. I learned to adjust my eyes to the kerosene lamp that Miss Myma lit so that I could read after nightfall. I learned to make sure that we got wood in to burn in the potbellied wood stove to warm the house in the cool mornings. I learned that if I filled a number-three tub with water from a neighbor's well in the morning and set it in the hot island sun all day, the water would be just the right temperature for a refreshing bath in the evening.

Miss Myma is a very sophisticated-looking woman, with high cheek bones, reddish brown skin that she says she acquired from the Wadmalaw Indians, and the most beautiful white hair I ever saw. She is naturally friendly, smokes a pipe, and is said to have been very lively in her younger days. She is soft-spoken and generally restrained in her language (though I have heard some of her women friends use words which would make the vulgarest of men shrink in shame). Her manner can be deceiving, however. I observed her once in an argument with

Miss Myma, who has lived her entire life on Wadmalaw Island, befriended
the author and introduced her to the ways of the island and its people.

one of her friends, who accused her of taking some tobacco which Miss Myma clearly could not have taken. Her friend attacked her viciously and called her some scandalous names. With each insult Miss Myma replied, "You de right, darlin," or "Sho will, honey," or "I know you ben tell truth for sho, baby." Finally, the friend looked rather foolish, throwing out insults and having them accepted so calmly. So, clearly feeling unfulfilled because she had not had the satisfaction of arousing Miss Myma to any angry word play, she left kicking up dust and looking back over her shoulder as she stalked down the sandy lane from Miss Myma's house. I had seen Miss Myma at her best in heated arguments over far smaller issues before; thus I asked her in amazement why she had not retaliated and defended herself forcefully. She took her pipe from her mouth, shook it in the direction her friend had taken, and replied thoughtfully that that particular woman was a fool, and she left fools in the hands of the Lord.

Miss Myma was apparently in her mid to late seventies when I met her. She told me that she "forget" how old she really was, but she could come close if I could tell her how old some of her childhood friends were. In spite of her age, she remains one of the most active people on the island. She taught me to crab, net, and fish. In fact, I caught my first dogfish while fishing on the banks of an island stream. The thing actually had feet and barked like a dog when I caught it on the hook. When I asked if the fish were edible, the children standing on the bank laughed at my ignorance before they said no.

Every day was an exciting day with Miss Myma. We got up around six o'clock and drove the fifteen or more miles to James Island to get a cup of coffee. Miss Myma liked to ride, and I loved the invigorating smell of the Sea Island morning air. If we were going to the creek that day, we would gather our gear beforehand. If we were going "bogging" for crabs, which was Miss Myma's preferred way to catch them, we would get our sticks and go to the creek after the tide had gone out. Bogging for crabs is hard work; one even needs specific shoes for this venture. When the tide goes out, many crabs are left in the various nooks and crannies of the creek bank and bed. The stick is used not only for support but to prod into holes to scare out the crabs. When one is found, it is provoked into clamping onto the stick and then pulled up and dropped into a large bucket. If the crab is ornery and refuses to clamp onto the stick, the stick is used to hold him down. He is picked up from the back and his two front claws are quickly clamped together;

then he is thrown into the bucket. In a good season one gets more crabs than one can eat in a couple of hours. If the season is bad, one can stay out in the creek all day in the sultry island sun and still have only a few "po, skase [scarce]" little crabs. During the bad seasons it was usually I and not Miss Myma who finally had to come in. She could walk miles in those creek beds. One day, when we had come upon a pool of water deeper than the regular creek bed, and thus not emptied by the tide, she decided she would teach me to throw a net. She stooped, pulled out her net, stationed part of the midpoint in her teeth, stretched a portion along her arm, circled the net a bit for balance, let go of the string, and twirled the net up over the small but deep hole of water. The net circled, fanned out, and landed on the pool. "Good throw, Miss Myma," I cried out. She replied, "Got em, a mullet for sho, Pat." It was true, she had netted several mullet, but what she didn't know was that she had netted a snake as well!

Crabbing can be dangerous for those unfamiliar with "ocean time." While one can bog for crabs when the tide goes out, one can net a few when the tide starts back in. I learned that the trickling sounds heard only at certain times are made when the nooks and crannies are being filled with water. I also learned that the tide can be deceiving because it comes in very slowly. Once we had been walking on the muddy creek floor for hours when I casually observed that the water was covering my shoes; a little later I noted that it was over my ankles. I thought I was just walking into deeper puddles and thus continued to practice my netting. Then I found that the water was beginning to hit me above my knees. Suddenly I became alarmed and looked back down the creek the way we had come. It was only then that I realized that the water was not only filling the creek bed but had covered the marshland, and there was no clearly perceivable way back to the higher ground. Frightened, I yelled out to Miss Myma that we were going to drown. She stopped, looked up and down the creek, pulled a bit of Day's Work chewing tobacco out of her pocket, took a good bite, offered me some, grinned when I passed on it, and finally said, "Guess time we fe go now." She had crabbed in that creek since she was a child, and she knew every bend and angle of it. Without her experience, however, I believe I would have panicked and perhaps drowned because it takes only minutes for the tide to rush in and fill the creek at any given point.

Miss Myma's presence was imperative at storytelling contests, whether held at Mr. Ted's store or in the clearing under the big Angel Oak tree behind her trailer. As noted before, Miss Myma always told the first tale at a preplanned storytelling, as a way of sanctioning the event. Really not much of a storyteller, she was more relaxed when a group of her "nipping" friends decided to tell "lies" at her house than at gatherings at Mr. Ted's store. The huge Angel Oak, with its ghostly hanging moss, shaded the ground so grass would not grow around it and thus helped to provide a clean, insect-free surface on which to relax. It also served as an anchor for Miss Myma's many respectable and some not-so-respectable friends, a place to sit, smoke, take little nips, and catch the breeze throughout the day. By late afternoon, when her respectable friends had long since gone to return to jobs, see about the children, or attend to chores, her not-so-respectable friends, not having to be responsible to anyone or anything, would settle in and ready themselves to tell lies throughout the night. Miss Myma's sleeping times remain a source of fascination for me. I could never understand how she managed to get up so early and go to bed so late. But then, many of the islanders are night people, roaming the highways, dancing, listening to music, and visiting friends in the dark. There were, however, occasions when Miss Myma actually got up and went to bed, leaving her friends still nipping under the oak.

In the winter of 1976 Miss Myma finally agreed to come to Michigan to visit me. She would not consent to fly; she would come only if I sent her a Greyhound bus ticket. I sent her the ticket and was delighted that she actually did come, and even more delighted that she would stay for three weeks. It was horribly cold in Michigan that year; Miss Myma did not care to go outside, and cared even less for the nine-degree-below-zero temperature and the mounds of snow. She preferred the warmth and comfort of sitting by the fireplace in our den, smoking her pipe. I was glad that we had a fireplace, and especially happy when she looked into the fire and began to reminisce and tell my two young children tales of Ber Rabbit. She gave them an oral tradition of tales in those three weeks that could not be matched with a lifetime of written literature. They were utterly fascinated by her. She knew my three-year-old daughter well not only because I had taken her with me to visit the Sea Islands but because on one of those occasions my daughter, who is asthmatic, had a severe attack around three in the morning. I had used all of her medicine, and there are no drugstores on Wadmalaw Island. Miss Myma observed her labored breathing for a while, and chastised me for not keeping an extra bottle of her medicine with me. Then she got up calmly, took her kerosene lamp, went out in the field behind her house, dug up some kind of root, brought it back, washed it, and boiled it. When the tea from the root had cooled, she took my wheezing daughter into her lap and coaxed her into drinking a cup of the reddish liquid. Twenty minutes later my daughter lay asleep and breathing peacefully on her lap.

In the fall of 1982 Miss Myma's trailer caught fire from her kerosene lamp and burned. Fortunately, she was not injured in the fire. She went to live with a relative whom she had raised as her daughter and who lived only a few doors away. Miss Myma is well into her eighties now. Her daughter told me that her mind wanders from time to time and that she has a tendency to wander off physically from home. In fact, she strayed down to the creek and was lost overnight at one point. A rescue squad was called in, but she was not found until the next morning when a helicopter pilot spotted her sitting out in the open field just beyond the creek banks. She was alert and did not suffer as much as a cold from the dampness and exposure. When I saw her most recently in the spring of 1985, she was sitting under the Angel Oak, a little nip in one hand to warm her blood, a crabbing stick in the other. She was smiling faintly and waving goodbye to me as I headed down the lane. She looked as if she were waiting for just the right moment to slip off down to the creek and nab a crab or catch a mullet "for sho."

*Ida Mae* is different from most of the women on the Sea Islands, very different. After having five children out of wedlock, and becoming a grandmother four times over by the time she was thirty-nine, she told me she had given up trying to be respectable in that community.

Ida Mae was an attractive woman when I met her in 1973. She had nut brown skin and flashing white teeth accented by a gold tooth that glistened in the sun when she laughed. She had the kind of face that was designed for the close-cut, boyish afro that she kept edged to perfection. Her light hazel eyes—"devil eyes," the islanders called them—were offset by her rich, dark color and gave the appearance of jumping out at you. She liked her eyes and said they were one of the reasons that she had had the gold tooth put in. In fact, when she first got it, she said, she used to practice smiling and turning her head just so the light would touch on her eyes, her tooth, and the large fourteen-karat gold hoop earrings that one of her men friends had given her. She had the dark full lips which some people call "blue lips" because of their defined darkness and smoothness. They are the kind of lips that never need lipstick, but I have seen her take one of her children's graphite pencils, scratch it against a surface to make the point soft and blunt, and rub it across her lips to accentuate their darkness. In spite of having had five children, she still had an excellent figure, and a figure is important to Sea Island men. Her rounded posterior filled out her jeans and made all of her clothes hang just right. She told me once that she was not sure it was an advantage to a woman to be built the way she was, because if she had not had, in her own words, "such a big ass," maybe the men would have left her alone, and she would not have got pregnant when she was fourteen. She reflected on that statement for awhile, took a long draw from her cigarette, and then amended it by saying, "Hell, who knows what I would have done?" She had always liked men as much as they seemed to like her, she finished by saying, and she probably would have got pregnant anyway.

I concluded that her attractiveness emanated not only from her looks but from her style and manner as well. She had a natural, inborn sophistication and presence that any *Vogue* model would envy. I showed her a copy of *Vogue* once, along with *Essence, Cosmopolitan,* and *Ebony,* and asked if she would like a complimentary subscription to one for Christmas. She flipped through *Vogue* and commented that she had no place to go to wear the kind of "shit" the models displayed; she browsed through *Essence* and said it had too much fancy cooking, and the only food that tasted good to her was cowpeas and bone; she read through *Cosmopolitan* and said it seemed to be about white women wanting sex, and hell, she got enough of that without reading about it. She finally settled on *Ebony* because she liked the pictures of Billy Dee Williams.

In spite of her language and outward hardness, there was something about Ida Mae that made her very feminine. Perhaps it was the way she held her cigarette, the way she walked, or the way she smiled just enough to show a glint of her gold tooth. Perhaps it was the coyness with which she captivated a man's attention, any man's, that made the more respectable women of the community dislike her and the more respectable men, especially the older ones, want to get close enough to her to smell her perfume, maybe inadvertently brush against her, or at least get into a position to see her back action as she walked away. I even overheard a deacon in the church comment to her one afternoon, while buying a soda at Mr. Ted's store, that she had on a mighty fine-looking dress and it was sho' hitting her in all the right places. She turned, gazed into his eyes just a split second longer than what was respectable, flipped a few ashes from her cigarette on his shiny black shoes, smiled ever so slightly, and walked away. He watched her as she moved out of his eyesight. Then he hitched up his pants, put both hands in his front pockets, and asked the Lord to give him strength.

Late one Saturday afternoon I walked up the lane past the Angel Oak behind Miss Myma's house to visit Ida Mae. She lived in a two-room shanty with three of her five children. The two older girls had lived with her mother since they were born. There were no children yelling and screaming outside, however, so I thought Ida Mae was not home. I started to leave when she popped her head out of her bedroom and said, "Hi, Pat." I was lonely, so I was glad to find her in. I asked her why it was so quiet, and where the children were. She said she sent them down to her mother's house to spend the night. When I asked her why, she replied, "Ain't you business, but I de spect company soon, and when he de come, you go have fe leave." I said that was okay. We sat on the broken steps in front of her shanty and chatted about general things, children, school, work, people on the islands.

She asked about my husband and if he didn't get jealous with me running around down there. I said I didn't think so, that I had really never given him a reason to be jealous. She replied that men never needed a reason to be jealous, that they were jealous by nature and it was to a woman's advantage to keep them that way. She asked what I was doing on the islands every year, and what Africa had been like, and if the men loved big-butt women there as much as men did here. I told her that I was trying to reconstruct Africanisms, and yes, the African men loved big-butt women as much as Sea Island men did. In fact, I told her that my female friends in Nigeria had teased me because my rear end was not as round as theirs, and I had retaliated by saying that was true for me, but the Sea Island women still had behinds that would put theirs to shame. She laughed and said she was glad I told the bitches that.

She offered me a cigarette. I thanked her but refused, saying I didn't smoke. Then she offered me a shot of whiskey; again, I thanked her but refused, saying I didn't drink. Then she offered me a joint; I thanked her and said I didn't smoke pot either, and wondered where she had got it. She turned, studied me a moment, and said, "You ain't de drink, ain't de smoke cigarette, ain't de dulge in pot. What de hell you do for fun? You de Jehovah Witness or something?" I laughed and told her I liked to travel, write, and come down there to visit her. She shook her head and replied that I must lead a sad life if coming down there was what I called fun.

As we sat talking and gazing out at the dusk and incoming fog, she asked me if I remembered the time I had gone with her to work in the field tying tomatoes. We laughed and reflected on that day. She had told me that if I really wanted to go I had to get up around six o'clock, put on some long pants and a long-sleeved shirt, and borrow one of Miss Myma's wide straw hats. I could hardly sleep that night thinking I would oversleep and miss the truck. Miss Myma woke me up, though, and cautioned me for the fifth time that it was too hot in the fields, that some people had had sunstrokes, and that I should stay there with her until Ida Mae came back in the evening. For the fifth time I said no, I wanted to go. When I arrived at Ida Mae's house dressed in my tomato-tying clothes, she grinned at me and asked if I had brought anything for lunch. I said no, so we walked down to Mr. Ted's store, and I bought some Vienna sausage and crackers. Then we stood by the highway until Dan Seabrooke came along in his truck and picked us up to drive us the ten or so miles to the tomato patch. Once we got there, we piled out and were each given strips of twine and told to take a row. I took one between Ida Mae and one of her friends because they felt that between the two of them, they could help me keep up.

Tying tomatoes is a monotonous, tiring, backbreaking job. Some of those rows were more than a mile long. A stick had been hammered into the ground to support each plant. We took the twine and tied the plant to the stick near the base, in the middle, and at the top. Each plant was about a foot from the next, and when we had tied one plant to its stick, we moved on to the next one, and the next one, and the next one, and the next one until we reached the end of the row. When we reached the end of one long row, we turned around and started back down another long row. It took a while for me to get the hang of what to do, and thus I found myself falling behind the others in the field. Ida Mae stopped tying her row and started tying my plants in front of me, so that when I got up to that point I could skip to where the rest of the people were. Around ten o'clock I was tying as fast as I could and sweating profusely. I did not think I could make it until noon and finish at least half a day, but Ida Mae told me if I could tie just until I reached the big Angel Oak down on the end it would be noon and I could rest. That consoled me. She said that when our shadow was directly under our feet on the row we were tying it would be twelve o'clock. When that happened, true enough, the whistle blew and we stopped, walked back to the truck, took turns getting cool drinks of water with a dipper from the cooler in back of the truck, got our lunches, sat down, ate, and rested.

One o'clock came only too quickly, three came too slowly, and five o'clock quitting time not quickly enough. The temperature rose to more than 103 degrees, and there was nothing between the sun and my head but Miss Myma's straw hat. I will always be grateful to Ida Mae for her help that day. She tied her row and most of mine, but I could at least tell Miss Myma that I had made a day! I would treasure that day and that ten dollars as among my most demanding achievements.

As we sat and continued to wait for Ida Mae's company, I reminded her of her summertime addiction to card playing. When she did not catch a truck to go to the fields, she spent the day, from sunup to sundown, with her card-playing buddies. They took turns buying a nipping bottle to help them get through the day. I met her when she came to play cards one day under the Angel Oak behind Miss Myma's house and Miss Myma took me out to meet her and her friends. I think I enjoyed these people more than any other group on the Sea Islands. When they played cards, they played for money, and for keeps. They invited me to play once; I accepted and lost twenty dollars my first game. After that, I just sat and listened. I learned that Ida Mae could outplay and outcurse any of the men. In addition, she could match them word for word playing the dozens. Once a card-playing friend asked her to scramble him some eggs for breakfast. She replied, "I ain't you wife." He said he knew that, but he still wanted some eggs. She answered, "I ain't you maid." He said he would pay her to cook them. She replied, "With what? I de win all you money." Then he said, "Well, I pay you with something else then." She answered, "You ain't got nothing else I de want." He said, "Well, you de come on and de go with me and you de see what I got." She burst into laughter and said, "What for I ben go with you, you ain't know what fe do with me if you de get me!"

Now we sat on in the dark. Eventually we saw the lights from a car coming up the lane; the car stopped in front of the shanty, and a tall attractive man got out and, as was customary, handed her a half gallon of ice cream as a gift. Since I already knew him, and also knew that he was another woman's man, I excused myself and walked back down the lane to Miss Myma's house.

A few years ago Ida Mae lost her mother, and a while later her father. As the oldest, she had to move back home to become the head of her extended family, according to traditional Sea Island practice. Among those who now needed her was John, a mentally retarded cousin around thirty-six or thirty-seven years old. She told me that the reason she could not accept a ticket to come and visit me was that she could not trust anyone else to take care of him. John frightened me when I first met him, not because he was retarded but because he was alert enough to know the value of money and, running out to my car when I drove up, grabbed my arm and demanded, "Quarter, quarter, quarter." He would not let go until someone had given him a quarter. Later I realized that was how he managed to have money to buy pop and ice cream whenever someone went to the store: everyone who came to Ida Mae's house had to give John a quarter. He was purported to keep them in socks, hidden somewhere around the house.

I last saw Ida Mae in the summer of 1984. She had lost weight and no longer had the old sassiness in her walk or devilishness in her eyes. After all, she has to take full responsibility for more than twelve people now, and surely that is enough to drain some of the spunk out of even the sassiest of women. Nevertheless, as she sat on her front porch fanning flies and rocking her new grandbaby, a gentleman drove up, got out of his car, and said that since it was "hot too much" out, he thought she might like a little ice cream to cool her off. She took a long draw from her cigarette, turned, gazed intently into his eyes, and smiled just enough for him to see the glint of her gold tooth.

I found that Ida Mae's presence served as a welcome catalyst for spontaneous, ribald storytelling. Although she was unbeatable at playing the dozens, she was not herself much of a storyteller. Because of her life-style she felt she was an outcast in the community. She seldom ventured far from home, unless she was going to work in the field; seldom associated with women other than those who played cards with her daily; and seldom attended church. Thus she had little opportunity to come in contact with language other than the creole, and as a result, her speech was more characteristic of contemporary Gullah than most.

*Ozzie Rivers, Mr. Hampy* (Happi), was a very religious, serious man who could sit for hours sermonizing and philosophizing about

God, roots, and life. He was respected in the community and renowned for his knowledge of the Bible and root medicine. He owned a
fair amount of land, which he put to good use growing corn, cucum-
bers, peas, okra, tomatoes, and other vegetables. The only time I ever
got to talk with him was late evenings (when the sun "de red for
down"), when he would come in from plowing and planting and sit
under his big pecan tree to "catch some breeze." On a few occasions
his wife, Miss Maime, a small, short-legged, soft-spoken woman,
brought his plate out to the pecan tree so that he could eat while he
talked to me. His plate had always been set aside and kept warm, and it
was indeed tempting, piled high with cowpeas and bone, a good helping of corn bread sliced and filled with fresh butter and molasses,
onions and tomatoes from the garden, and hot pepper sauce, with
penny drink or iced tea served in his own particular glass.

Mr. Hampy was not a lonely man. He had several children and
more head of grandchildren than he felt he could keep up with. Mr.
Hampy's children who had remained at home had built their houses or
set up their trailers so that each shared the communal yard area near his
home, as is traditional in Sea Island family communities. Some of his
children, including a special daughter, had moved to New York. The
daughter was special because she had been born with a caul over her
face and was thus thought to have the gift not only to see ghosts, hants,
or hags but to be able to know things that other people are not privileged to know. Mr. Hampy himself had been born with a caul, and he
was thus able to sympathize with her special sight. In fact, he attributed her leaving the island and going to New York in part to her
desire for an area where such things as ghosts, hags, and plat-eyes
were less prevalent. Because the island roads are densely forested, they
are judged natural haunts for the spirits of the dead. Mr. Hampy often
amused himself by telling me that if I really wanted to see a ghost, he
could show me one any day of the week just after midnight on the road
leading to the Presbyterian graveyard. However, we never made that
journey after nightfall to see the ghost standing at the entrance to the
lane (see Appendix 3).

Mr. Hampy told no tales of Ber Rabbit and his witty ways, though
he admitted that he knew many of them. His only topics were religious
or medicinal. It was from him that I learned many of the Sea Island
folk cures. He accompanied me to the wooded area behind his home
and pointed out some of the common roots that grow on top of the

ground: dog fennel, sea muckle, and mullein, all of which can be dried, boiled, and made into teas to alleviate ailments like colds, stuffy noses, headaches, and nervous conditions. In addition, he pointed out several varieties of the more potent underground roots: white root, known to relieve headaches and cold symptoms; black root, said to be good for nerves and the shakes; snakeroot, excellent for constipation; and the revered bloodroot, said actually to bleed when it is cut and generally accepted even by the younger generations as a cure for such blood disorders as anemia and high and low blood pressures and for various female problems. I was privileged to be offered samples of some of his many medicinal cures, for example, snakeroot boiled and steeped for four months in good whiskey. Though this concoction is bitter and among the worst-tasting of all the herbal cures, it is fairly common on Sea Island shelves. Some say, "If the taste ain't de move whatever de pain you, the whiskey sho will." Mr. Hampy believed that when one took something from nature, like a root, one had to return something back to it. Thus for every root he dug up he left a few cents in the hole, more or less depending on the type of root; only silver money, for example, was left for the bloodroot.

Mr. Hampy's oral style was typical of most Sea Island religious oratory, though, since he was accustomed to public address on Sundays as well as storytelling, his language varied according to the occasion. In telling his religious tales, he would engage his audience's attention with the seriousness of his subject and the dignity of his manner. Unlike Mr. Henry, he seldom stood. He would begin very slowly, explaining that his subject matter could always be substantiated by the Bible (though in some cases, as it turns out, it could not be). In the midst of his sermon or tale, he would often do as Miss Deeley did: stop, look around at each of the listeners' faces, and say, "I ain't believe you know what I ben talk about, do you?" Not expecting a reply, he would continue. The question was to gauge the extent to which he held his audience's attention. Whether he had everyone's attention or not, he, like Mr. Henry, would proceed to talk until I ran out of tape, until it was too dark, or until the mosquitoes became too bad to continue to sit outside.

During one of my recent trips to the Sea Islands, in the summer of 1984, Mr. Hampy died. His doctors said that there was no medical reason why he should have died. According to the islanders, Miss Maime, his wife, had been battling cancer for more than ten years and had often been hospitalized for short periods for her condition. She finally lost the battle or, as some islanders said, she finally won the battle, staked her sword in the golden sand, and went home to the Kingdom of God on 4 July 1984. Mr. Hampy was told, and he died the next day, 5 July. Some said that the couple had been together so long that his spirit had become a part of hers and that when she died, he died simply because he lacked the will to live without her. Others commented that since her body remained warm so long after her death, she was waiting for him to follow.

Their funeral was one of the most elaborate I have seen in the Sea Island area. The cost was well in excess of fifteen thousand dollars, a total which the couple had prepared for over the years by paying on their funeral policy. They had matching blue caskets with intricate gold designs. Hers was covered with a spread of pink flowers, his with a spread of blue ones. The undertaker was careful with such details as having her coffin brought in first and stationing her coffin to the left of his. These were things that the viewers would observe and remember when they selected someone to handle their own funeral arrangements.

The Presbyterian church was packed beyond capacity, and I stood outside the door of the church along with other friends hoping to see the couple one last time. Two male associates had accompanied me to the funeral and stood among the other men on the church ground, chatting. As a female, I knew that I was not permitted this liberty. Women do not stand outside the church and chat when services are going on. If they cannot get inside the church, they stand as close to it as possible or remain in their cars. In a break with custom, the caskets were not opened for viewing the bodies; I walked with others more than two miles up a long, narrow, muddy lane to the gravesite, still hoping to see their faces. However, before I made it up the lane, they had passed the younger children over the caskets to prevent their spirits from being "touched" by the spirits of the dead. As is traditional, they buried Mr. Hampy and Miss Maime side by side, she on his left, in a densely wooded area to help enclose their spirits. Each grave was covered with flowers and clocks were set at the time each one died.

Placing a clock on the grave of the deceased to depict the hour of death is still a strong tradition.

## Conclusion

Folktales, like languages, are not immutable. They are constantly changing: the plots vary, the characters change, new names are substituted for old ones, and the language of the tales generally takes on the flavor and style characteristic of the era; any given speaker may rearrange, improvise, or improve a plot, episode, or character to his own specifications. On the Sea Islands the teller may add such things as telephones, highways, automobiles, and even televisions in contemporary tales, yet these innovations are set within the framework of traditional themes. In the minds of some island youngsters, for example, Ber Rabbit may now live in a house instead of his traditional hollow in the briar patch. But plots remain essentially the same: Ber Rabbit still tricks Ber Wolf, but instead of returning to his den in the hollow, he returns to his house in or near a briar patch.

While the speakers may vary in their individual styles of delivery, there remain very distinct features characteristic of Sea Island folk telling:

The teller
1. will usually tease his audience when he has them thoroughly involved in his tale by pretending to forget or pretending that he will finish his tale at a later time;
2. will usually ask rhetorical questions of given members, and will expect one member or all members of his audience to respond;
3. will usually try to make his delivery as dynamic and emotional as possible through modulations in the pitch or tone of voice;
4. will usually speak louder and more rapidly when he begins to close his narration;
5. will usually make his closing as dramatic as possible;
6. will usually give a tale a moral if one is not already inherent;
7. will usually use a range of kinesic movements or gestures to help describe the events of a tale.

The audience
1. will usually respond or reply to questions or cues given by a speaker;

2.  will usually respond overtly to a good storyteller by injecting words of praise or understanding such as "Yeah," "That's right," or "I know what you mean" during the entire course of a tale;
3.  will usually expect the performer to end with a dynamic closing and express their appreciation of his tale by saying, "That's all right" or "You sure enough know how for tell good tale";
4.  will usually harmonize the rate, rhythm, pitch, and loudness of their responses to accord with those of the performer;
5.  will usually communicate with people nearby either nonverbally, through head nods, handshakes, approving or disapproving glances, or other communicative techniques, or verbally, through words and phrases like "You hear what he de say," "Yeah, man!" and others.

The storyteller is only one of the ingredients necessary for seeing and hearing a good tale. The tradition dictates that the storyteller cannot perform alone. Not only must he be in a place conducive to telling a good tale, but he must have an interested and responsive audience in order to do his best performing. When all these ingredients are mixed in proportion, the performances of both the teller and the listeners are commensurate with traditional Sea Island social practices. The dependence of one on the other remains as apparent in everyday interactions on the Sea Islands as it does in the African cultures of the Igbo, Yoruba, Ibebio, and others from which the Sea Islanders are descended and from whose folktales their stories are said to have been derived.

# 3

---

# The Texts

## The Prayers

My knee ben down on cold cold floor!

The prayers are the most creative and expressive form of Sea Island oratory. Like the tales, they are composed and delivered within a set tradition, but the success of the delivery is dependent not only on what the speaker says but also on the eloquence and rhetorical skill with which he says it. To the Sea Island congregation, outstanding rhetorical skills are attributes to be praised, practiced, and deeply venerated as essential characteristics of learned people. The learned people, however, are frequently those without much academic background. Without a doubt, many of the best expositors of the prayer tradition have little, if any, formal education. Their prayers, nevertheless, are composed in a tradition of impassioned eloquence. They embody Ciceronian, Quintilianesque, and other ornaments of style capable of creating belief, inspiring, and passionately persuading a congregation to respond with raucous and joyous replies.[1]

Both men and women, but only those known to be carriers of the prayer-giving tradition, pray at specified times during the church service. The member called on will kneel and pray publicly without pausing, stuttering, or searching for words for as long as twenty-five minutes, depending on the occasion for the prayer. The ability to pray is considered a "gift" like the ability to sing or play the piano. Those gifted with the technique are singled out when they are very young and encouraged to practice speaking in the church at special feasts, weddings, or holidays, especially Easter and Christmas. As children they learn only to speak the words; as adults they know how to speak them with the compassion that comes only from experience. Others may acquire the ability to join in the words of prayer, but only those who have the gift can move the congregation to shout out a response.

None of the prayers are written, and herein lies much of their inventiveness. Many rival T. S. Eliot's *Wasteland* in elaborate allusions to works of literature. The most effective ones are alive with imagery, maxims, puns, understatements, and cultural references which the audience understands and responds to enthusiastically. More important, the prayers are filled with devices used judiciously throughout to induce the rhythmic incantation that is imperative to the Sea Island prayer tradition. Alliteration, transplacement, interplacement, epanaphora (repetition of words or phrases at the beginning of successive clauses), and other features create pleasing recurrent sounds which stir, stimulate, and evoke verbal responses from the audience. Epanaphoric passages—for example, "I want to be the child of God! / and I want my sins forgiven / I want my spirit meek and mild / and I want to go to Heaven when I die"—add to the beauty of the prayers and also demonstrate the speaker's skill as a rhetorician. The echoes of words and phrases in the audience's responses attest to the community's respect and admiration for skillful and creative use of language:

Master, it's no lower    *No! No lower!*
Could I come this evening
Excepting my knees are down at the floor    *Floor! Cold floor!*
Guilty heart within
Crying guilty and already condemned    *Condemned!*

Alliteration is used, as in "coax and call," "cold, cold hearts," and "Holy Spirit, heavenly Dove," to help establish the rhythm, as well as to contribute to the enthusiastic and energetic tone of the entire delivery.

The strong rhythm and chanted delivery of the prayers accords with the prayer traditions of many African and African-derived cultures, including those of West Africa, the West Indies, and South America. The rhythmic chants are crucial to the developmental flow of the prayers.[2] Once the rhythm is established, it is maintained through various means, most important of which is the reply from the listeners. Some truly impressive prayer givers excite an audience to maximal response through their energetic diction and explosive tone alone. Others may intensify the rhythmic effect by drumming with a chair, tapping a cane against the floor, or just swaying back and forth in time to some inaudible sound.[3]

It has been suggested that some respondents in African-American congregations may not understand or actually accept what the speaker says but respond instead to the highly contagious cadence established by the call from the speaker and response from the audience.[4] This observation may be justified in part: one may not be stimulated to respond to the message in the prayer, but it is difficult if not impossible to ignore the rhythm with which the prayer is delivered. Without a doubt, however, some congregants listen carefully to every detail—not only to receive the message but because, seeing that the prayers are not written, potential prayer givers must be attentive in order to learn the art of the prayer tradition.

Perpetuating this tradition is made easier by the formulaic element in their arrangement. They usually begin with a quotation from the Bible, a poem, or, more traditionally, some lines from the Lord's Prayer. The speaker usually has no prior knowledge that he will be asked to pray. Thus, the quotation gives him time to organize his thoughts and prepare himself to deliver an effective prayer. He is at liberty to alter a quotation to his own specification and often the alteration is more effective than the original. For example, the lines "For thine is the kingdom / The power and the glory" may be improved to "O Lord, that thine may be our kingdom / We expecting your kingdom to be / [a] poor sinner['s] glory!"

After the quotation, the speaker begins his personal prayer, a structured oration with a proem, line of appeal, and peroration. The proem opens with a rhetorical salutation to God commensurate with the solemnity of the occasion. It permits the speaker to express his humility as a servant of God, using such words as *mutable* and *impermanent*. The speaker does not presume to be as fortunate as the "foxes of the forest" or "the birds of the air." He projects himself as a mere waif asking for mercy with his knees bent in supplication:

Master Jesus, hear me
Another one of you[r] servant
Bow this evening, Jesus

Sin anguished and bended

. . . . . . . . . . . . . . .

Crying to you this evening, Jesus
For Mercy

While mercy can reach [us]

As you say the foxes of the forest
Got hole

And then the birds of the air has nest
Master, we are poor son of man

Nowhere to lay down weary head

The rhythm and tone are usually set in the speaker's salutation to God, after which the speaker begins his appeal. This plea is in the form of an itemized list. The number of requests will depend on the occasion and the number of items concerning which the speaker is asking for consideration. If he makes an appeal for himself, he usually includes it as the very last item in his list. Each appeal will often begin with a traditional expression, such as "Then, then, my God! We ask . . ." or "O! You, you this evening, my heavenly Father, we ask . . ." The pleas are likewise concluded with a traditional expression, like "Have Mercy if thou on us so please!" In addition to clarifying the organization of the prayers, these phrases, perhaps more than others, help to sustain the increasing force and rhythm.

The peroration may vary. Most prayers, however, end with the quotation "Somewhere Lord, Job declare / The weak shall cease in trouble and the soul find rest."

The Sea Islanders have prayers for every occasion. They may range from a one-minute request for assistance in the completion of a hard day of labor to a twenty-five-minute eulogy for a lost loved one. The first prayer quoted below was delivered for the 1980 Usher's Anniversary at New Jerusalem AME Church on Wadmalaw Island, South Carolina, and is typical of most Sea Island prayers for special occasions. In this case there was a scheduled prayer giver, but the person who actually spoke did so without notice when the scheduled speaker proved unavailable.[5] A brief outline of the prayer is included to demonstrate the smoothness and cohesiveness with which the parts develop into the whole:

I.   Formal opening

II.  The Lord's Prayer

III. Proem: speaker's personal prayer of humility

Master Jesus, hear me
Another one of you[r] servant

IV. Appeals

    A. Father, we down here this evening
       Heavenly Father
       Asking for your mercy

    B. We want you to come in this building
       One more time

    C. We ask you to please strengthen us
       Where we are weak
       And build us where we are tearing down

    D. We ask you to look at the leaders
       From one to another, Jesus
       Make them ushers of sound judgment
       Then truly devoted to God

    E. I want you to bless each and every usher
       Jesus
       Help them to please hold out and hold on

    F. Look at Reverend Pinckney one more time

    G. Look at the mistress of ceremonies
       Jesus

    H. Want you to look at Jerusalem one more time

    I. [Look at] me too

V. Peroration

       Somewhere, Lord, Job declare
       The wicked must cease in trouble
       And my soul have rest
       'Tis thy servant's prayer, Master!

The social setting in which a prayer of this sort is delivered contributes to the development of bilingual skills for many Gullah speakers. This prayer, like most others, contains few features characteristic of contemporary Gullah speech, such as the use of the preverbal markers *de, ben, bina,* and *don* and the omission of inflectional markers. There is a good reason for the absence of these and other features in this text. A prayer of this type is composed in a tradition of rhetorical eloquence and skill. Thus the speech is expected to be elevated and elaborate while retaining certain syntactic and phonological features characteristic of the community language. Many prayers are composed of hymns, Scriptures, spirituals, and traditional expressions, reflecting both biblical concepts and the black experience. Accordingly, the vocabulary, syntax, and phrasing do not necessarily represent those of the person praying, but may be words and phrasing he has heard and stored in his memory over the years. Again, the learned prayer givers are most often those "gifted" in the art, with little formal training. The important factors are that the person have a good memory, be able to join beautifully constructed phrases together spontaneously, and be able to establish a chanting rhythm which can be easily sustained by the reply from the audience. While the text alone is intelligible on paper, most of the beauty of the prayer escapes, along with the force of the audience's reply and the increasing fervor of the speaker's call.

## Opening Prayer for the Usher's Anniversary

Mr. James Brown
New Jerusalem AME Church
Wadmalaw Island, South Carolina
13 July 1980

> Our Father, who art in heaven
> Hallowed be thy name
> Thy kingdom come, O Lord
> Let thy holy and righteous
> will be done on this earth
> As you will was already done in heaven
> Give us, Lord, this day
> As our daily bread
> You forgive those who have sin
> And trespass against us    *Amen*
> Lead us not into sin, neither temptation
> But, please deliver us from evil    *Yes!*
>
> O Lord, that thine may be our kingdom
> We expecting your kingdom to be
> [A] poor sinner['s] glory    *Oh yeah!*

Master Jesus, hear me
Another one of you[r] servant
Bow this evening, Jesus   *Bow, yes! My Lord!*

Sin anguished and bended   *Bended knees*

Master, it's no lower
Could I come this evening   *No! No lower!*

Excepting my knees are down at the floor   *Floor! Cold floor!*

Guilty heart within
Crying guilty and already condemned   *Condemned*

Crying to you this evening, Jesus
For MERCY[6]   *Yeah. Uh hum*
While mercy can reach [us]
As you say the foxes of the forest   *Yes*
Got hole[7]

And then the birds of the air has nest   *Yes!*
Master, we are poor son of man   *Pray now!*

Nowhere to lay down weary head   *Yeah!*

Father, we down here this evening   *Oh yeah!*

Heavenly Father
Asking for your mercy
While mercy can reach us
Father, while traveling over the mortal   *Yes, oh yeah*
Vineyard this afternoon[8]
We ask you to please drop water here   *Yes*

Don't leave us alone to ourself   *Uh uh*

Neither in the hands of the wicked man   *Ah yeah!*

Lead us though in the tempting of old Satan[9]   *Oh yeah!*
Have mercy if thou on us so please.
We are here this evening, Jesus   *Oh yeah. Uh huh. Oh yeah*

We can't do nothing without you
Come Holy Spirit, heavenly Dove[10]
With all thou quickening power   *Power!*

Kindle the flame of our Savior love   *Yeah!*

In these cold hearts of ours    *Cold*

Master, look how we are groveling here below    *Oh yeah! All*
    *right. Yeah*
Trying to find our earthly toys
Master, our poor soul can't find a goal
But we trying to reach an eternal joy[11]    *Joy*

Have mercy, if thou only so please    *So please*

And then, then, my God    *My Lord*

While traveling from Jericho
Maybe going to Jerusalem    *Uh hum*
We want you to come in this building    *Yes*
One more time
Want you to touch us this evening, Jesus    *Yes*
Realize this evening, Father    *Oh yeah*
We are nothing but a chaff before the wind[12]    *Before the wind*

We get raindrop in the morning
Just as bloom of the lily
By noon we cut off, wilt and die    *Die! Oh Yeah*

Have mercy, if thou only so please
And then, then, my God    *My God*

You know the purpose of our gathering
Jesus    *Yes*

We ask you to please strengthen us
Where we are weak    *Oh yeah*
And build us where we are tearing down[13]    *Tearing down*

Here we are trying to celebrate this twentieth anniversary,
    Jesus    *Oh yeah*
Give us faith that will not shrink    *Mercy!*

But oppressed by every folding
And then, then, my God    *Then, my God! Oh yeah!*

We ask you to look at the leaders    *Oh yeah!*
From one to another, Jesus    *Yes*
Make them ushers of sound judgment

Then truly devoted to God
We realize, heavenly Father    *Yes*
From, from July last gone    *Oh yeah*

What trouble have I seen?    *Yes. Oh yeah*

What conflict have I bear?
Sometime I ben fighting within[14]    *Yeah*

And fear without
Since I assembled last    *Yes!*
Then, then, my God    *My God!*

I want you to bless each and every usher
Jesus[15]    *Uh hum. Yes*

Help them to please hold out and hold on    *Oh yes!*
Help them to follow building a household of God    *Yes, Lord!*
And then, then, my God    *Then!*

Help them not to wear a uniform
To be seen
But only to be a child of God    *God!*

Help them to say
I want to be the child of God    *Pure heart!*

And then, then, I want my sins forgiven    *Oh yeah!*

Want my spirit meek and mild    *Uh hum. Oh yeah!*

I want to get to heaven when I die
Do show me, Lord, thy way.    *Oh yeah!*

And then guide me on thy road    *Oh yeah. Oh Lord*

And then, then, my God
Never to let me go astray    *Astray*

Until I get home to thee    *Yes Lord!*

And then, then, heavenly Father    *Oh yeah*

Look at Reverend Pinckney one more time    *Oh yeah!*
Who is going [to] unfold the word of eternal truth    *Oh yeah!*
Want you to please, dear Jesus

Give him a silver trumpet[16]    *Uh huh!*
[So] he can coax and call some more ushers into this fold    *Oh
    yes!*
And then, then, then, my Master    *My Lord!*
Look at the mistress of ceremonies
Jesus    *Oh yeah!*
Want you to plant her deep down in the soil, Master    *Oh yeah!*
Where she'll never be [up]rooted by the storm of life[17]    *Oh
    yeah!*
Then, then, my God    *My God*

Want you to look at Jerusalem one more time    *Oh yeah!*
Help them to say
Jerusalem my happy home    *Yes! yes Lord!*
So never dear to me[18]    *Oh yeah!*
And then, then, Jesus    *Uh huh!*
Then, then, Lord    *Amen!*
Then, Master Jesus    *Oh yeah*

[Look at] me too got to pull off mortal    *That what you got to do.
    Oh yeah!*

Put on mortality[19]
Because then, Jesus
Going down by the river of Jordan    *Jordan*

Gonna stake my sword in the golden sand    *Oh yeah*

Because, Master Jesus    *Master Jesus!*

Wouldn't had to study war no more.[20]    *Oh yeah!*

And then, Lord    *Lord!*

I can hear her say    *All right*
Must I be that judgment bar    *Must I be*

Answer in thy day    *Oh yeah!*

Every vain or idle thought
And for every word I say    *Say now!*

For every secret of my heart    *O yeah!*
Will shortly be made known

And then, Lord    *Then Lord!*

I will go home and get
My just resolve[21]    *Oh yeah!*

For all that I have done    *Done!*

And then, Lord    *My Lord*

Want you to meet me, Jesus
Somewhere, Lord, Job declare    *Oh yeah!*

The wicked must cease in trouble    *Trouble!*

And my soul have rest[22]    *Rest*

'Tis thy servant's prayer, Master!

    Amen.    *Amen! Amen! Yeah! Yeah sir! All right!*


Mr. Mike Simmons was well into his nineties when Miss Myma introduced me to him and his wife (he has since died). He sat in the doorway of his two-room shanty and tolerated a seven-day linguistic procedure. I collected a phoneme inventory from him by asking him to pronounce nearly three hundred words. The task is slow and exacting; sometimes his wife, in her late eighties, would call out from the kitchen and offer a variant way in which a word could be pronounced. This was a lovely couple.

When Mr. Mike tired of the procedure, he would look out over the grassy field in front of his home and begin to hum an old-time song, or he would begin to pray. When he did either of these things, it was my cue that he was tired and I should leave. The following is one of his short prayers.

## The Lord's Prayer

Most Revered Mr. Mike Simmons
Wadmalaw Island, South Carolina
July 1976

> Our Father, who art in heaven
> Hallowed be thy name, thy kingdom come
> Thy will be done on earth as was done in heaven.
> Give us this day, O daily bread
> And forgive those who art in trespass against thee
> O heavenly Father!
> We are meeting on worldly soil today
> Calling on your name
> And, heavenly Father, couldn't do nothing until you come
> Come now, Jesus, if you please?
> The revered thanks to you today, heavenly Father
> O Lord, if you please!
> Look upon me in the eyes of pity
> In the heart of compassion
> I be so please, heavenly Father
> O Lord, from last August, the single
> They told us at least
> O heavenly Father, you know when fall down, get up
> Ben calling on your name
> And I couldn't do nothing until de come!
> Come now, heavenly Father, please, if you please
>
> Amen!

Tom Mack is an active member of the Wadmalaw church community. He is a professional singer and is considered well on his way to perfecting the prayer-giving tradition. Though he is in his early forties, he is, according to the islanders, still experiencing the "scalding water" of life, one of the primary ingredients in learning to chant the words of the prayers with emotion. When he heard that I was writing a book, he came by to see me and offered the following prayer for me to complete.

Prayer for Patricia Jones-Jackson

Thomas Mack, Sr.
Wadmalaw Island, South Carolina
July 1980

God, the sun is almost down
And the evening shall appear
O may we all remember well
The night of death draw near
We lay our garment by
Upon our bed to rest
But soon death will soon rob of all
Of what we here possess
At this evening
Thy heavenly Father
Hear me a moment
A creature bowed

This evening, Jesus
I ask you this evening
My heavenly Father    *Yes Lord!*
Remember Wadmalaw once more time
This evening, Jesus    *Yes Lord!*
Remember our community
This evening, Jesus
Remember Jerusalem
This evening, Jesus
We need you
This evening, Jesus
We are down here
In the lonesome valley
This evening
And we cannot do nothing
Until you come
Come, Holy Spirit
heavenly Dove
With all thy quiverling power
Kindle the flame

Of savior love
In these cold heart of ours
This evening, Jesus
O—O—O—You this evening
My God!
I ask you to remember
This young lady
If you only so please
This evening, Jesus
Remember sister Jackson
If you only so please
This evening, Jesus
Help her to write her book
This evening, O God!
That some might understand
This evening, Jesus
O—O—O—You this evening
My God!
Ride on the four corner
Of the world
This evening, Jesus
Ask you to remember
Her parents one day to the other
Help them up on every leaning side
This evening, Jesus
Build them up
Where torn down
This evening, O God!
Brace they back
Against the wall of Zion
And turn they head
Toward heaven side
If you only so please
. . . . . . . . . . . . .
This evening, Jesus

## A Sermon

For true, the Lord ben give em silver trumpet,
and he shonuf know how for blow em!

     The Reverend Renty Pinckney is minister of New Jerusalem AME Church on Wadmalaw Island, South Carolina. His sermon is not presented in its entirety here, because it is very long. The Reverend Mr. Pinckney, like most island ministers, has memorized the Bible thoroughly; his creativity is revealed by his ability to join scattered allusions into a cohesive whole.[23]

### The Bread of Life

Rev. Renty Pinckney
New Jerusalem AME Church
Wadmalaw Island, South Carolina
July 1980

God is the Bread of Life
God will feed you when you get hungry    *Oh yes! I know he will.*
   *All right! Yeah. Amen! Yes sir!*

Look on the mountain
Beside the hill of Galilee    *My Lord!*

Watch his disciple
Riding on the sea    *Yeah! Uh huh!*

Tossing by the wind and rain    *Yeah. Come up*

Going over the sea of temptation    *Uh hum*

Brother, I don't know
But I begin to think
In this Christian life    *Yes!*

Sometime you gone be toss    *Yes, yeah!*

By the wind of life    *Yes, my Lord!*

The wind gonna blow you
From one side to the other    *Yes!*

On this Christian journey

The way ain't gone be easy on us children    *No!*

And the disciple as they was going across    *Oh yes sir! Yeah.*

The wind was tossing
As they was going over to Cana    *All right! Uh hum*

The King was on the safe [same] side
To the Sea of Galilee    *All right*

To the land Gothen
It was so sufficient size
To be call a city    *Yeah, right! Yeah*
It was close to the seashore    *Shore. Yes*

One half mile long
Quarter of a mile wide    *Yes sir!*

Brother, I know
Jesus would be so glad    *So pleased!*

There he was among them
Brothren of our Lord
And his disciple    *Yes! Yes sir. Oh yes*

The Gospel!
Of John was formed in writing    *Writing*

Jesus was towhead    *All right*

They begin to wonder brother    *Yeah!*
How is this could be    *Yeah!*
We left him on the other shore    *Yeah*
But this morning we are here    *Yes, here. My Lord!*

Jesus don't have a boat    *Boat.*

Don't have a airplane    *Ah hah! Yeah!*

Here he are on the bank this morning    *Yes sir*

Yea God!   *Yeah God! Amen!*

What a fortune
All the power in he hand   *Oh Yeah!*
Got power for we   *Yeah*
When we get hungry   *Yeah*
He's able to feed us   *Yes sir*

O Lordy!
Come to tell you children   *Yes!*
Jesus! is the Bread of Life   *Jesus!*

My brothren   *My God!*
Come to him   *All right!*
Come to him   *Yeah!*
He feed you when you get hungry   *All right. Oh yeah!*

He will be on the ark   *Yeah!*

Yea God!   *My God*

Upon the montain someone said
Jesus said   *Yeah!*

If you come to me
I'll give you water   *Water*

In dry land   *Dry land!*

O Lordy!
Jesus is the Bread of Life   *Yes!*

How do you know   *Uh huh!*

He's the Bread of Life?   *Yeah!*

When he begins to speak   *Yeah!*

He's the Bread of Life, brothren   *Yeah!*

O Lordy!
I begin to think back   *Yeah!*

In Moses time
when he said   *Yeah!*

God feed them   *Oh yeah!*

With manna from on heaven
My brother!   *All right, yeah!*

I was out in the wilderness
Didn't had nothing to eat   *Uh huh*

God feed them   *My Lord!*

With manna from on high   *Yes!*

To stop a little while

(Pause)

I be able to preach for you   *Yeah! All right*

If you feed me with that bread   *Yeah! All right*

I be able to call him   *Yeah*

If you feed me with that bread   *Yes*

O Lordy!   *Oh Lord!*

I be able to book up   *Yeah! All right*

Pick up my brother   *Yes!*

Who is down in the ditch this morning   *Oh yeah!*

If you feed me this morning   *Yes! Lord*

I be able to call   *Yeah Lord*

The lost sinner home   *Yeah!*

O Lordy!
Jesus!
Is the Bread of Life   *Yeah*

God knows
Somebody look   *Yes*

Back in space of time   *Yes!*

Saw Jesus
Coming through
Seventy-two generations   *Yes. Uh huh*

One  said
When he look at Jesus    *Oh yes!*

Yea God!    *Yea God!*

His feet    *All right*

Look like polish brass    *Yeah!*

Eye look
Like a consuming fire    *Consuming fire*

Hair look
Like lamb wool    *Lamb wool*

Pressing the wine press    *Yeah!*

All by himself    *By himself*

Coming down to the gate    *Yeah!*

To let you and I
Have a right    *Right*

To the Tree of Life
O Lordy!    *Oh Lordy!*

Jesus is alive    *All right!*

My brothers    *Yes!*

When I get hungry    *Ah yeah!*

My soul get hungry
I go to Him    *Yeah. All right!*

And say unto Him    *Yeah. That's right!*

God I want you
Feed me with the Bread of Life    *Yes!*

Feed me    *Feed me!*

Til I want no more    *Want no more!*

Then at last    *At last!*

In this old world    *Yes! This old world. Thank you! At last. Yes
    sir. Step right on up. All right*

(Long pause)

Brother, I don't know about you, friend   *Yes*

But I begin to sing   *Yeah!*

Deep down in my heart   *All right! Sir!*

But Jesus is the Bread of Life   *Uh huh! All right*

Great God!   *Yes!*

Some how   *Some how. Yeah!*

Some way   *Some way!*

That same Jesus   *That same Jesus!*

One day   *Yes!*

I Look down   *Yes sir! Yeah!*

Into the old pit   *All right!*

A little wretch
Like me was
My brother   *Yeah!*

Stoop down   *Stoop down!*

And lift me up   *Lift me up!*

Take my feet
Out of the mucky mire   *Yeah!*

Climb up on
Rock of eternal ages
Establish my goings   *Yeah! Yeah!*

Say unto me   *Amen!*

I want you   *All right!*

To go out into the world   *Yeah!*

Tell man and women   *Yeah!*

I said
I was dead
But I'm alive, brothren   *I'm alive!*

Tell them I said    *Yeah. All right!*

When they get hungry    *Yeah!*

If they would come to me    *Yeah!*

I would feed them    *I will feed them. Yes!*

Tell them I said    *Yes*

When they get lonely
Don't have a friend    *A friend*

I will be a friend for them    *Yeah*

Tell them I said    *Yeah*

When all bodies    *Yeah*
Walk off from them
And put he name on every milepost    *Oh Lord!*

I'll be right there with them    *Yeah!*

Tell them I said    *Yeah! Yeah!*

When mother, father
Forsake you    *Oh yeah*

I be by your side    *By your side*

O Lordy!
And when you come    *Come, Jesus!*

To the end of your journey    *Yeah!*

And you are weary    *Weary!*

Of life my brother    *Yeah!*

Old battle is won    *Won!*

I'll be right there    *Be right there!*

When the time come
My God almighty!    *My Lord*

Gonna call the Angel    *Yeah!*

Take care    *Oh yeah!*

I want you to
Stand around    *Oh yeah!*

The throne this morning    *Oh yes*

Want you to sing    *Yeah!*

As you ever sing before
Somebody who will come out    *Yeah!*

From Jerusalem    *Yeah!*

Crying out
I know    *All right!*

Back yonder    *Yonder*

In yonder world    *Yonder world*
I cry some Sunday

A charge    *Jesus! A charge I have! Right*

To glorify    *Glorify!*
My brother    *My brother!*

I don't know
But I look across
In the amen corner    *Corner*

See somebody    *Yeah!*

Who cry out
One day    *Yeah!*

I saw the lighthouse    *Yeah! Oh yeah*

O Lordy!    *My Lord*

I wanna be there!    *Oh yeah!*

I wanna be there!    *Oh yeah! Oh yeah!*

I wanna be there!    *Oh yes! I wanna be there!*

Over yonder

(Long pause)

I wanna view the beauty land
Where God eternal glory    *Eternal glory!*

Where all wicked     *Wicked*

Shall cease     *Cease, cease! Yes Lord!*

All weary soul     *All weary soul!*

Shall be at rest     *Rest!*

Jesus said
I am the Bread     *I am the Bread. The Bread. I am the Bread*
Of Life

Let us Pray     *All right! Yes sir! Yes Lord! Let us pray!*
. . . . . . .


## Gullah Tales Exemplifying Audience Participation

RIDDLER: Round like a top. Deep like a cup.
Mississippi river ain't full em up!

RESPONDENT: A sifter (strainer)

The reply from the audience is as germane to the Sea Island tales as it is to the prayers and sermons. However, the relaxed social atmosphere in which tales are told permits more exchange between speaker and listener than does the more orthodox surroundings of the prayers and sermons. The storytellers are not set apart from the group by a sacred podium or some other feature used to separate participating service members from the rest of the group. The listeners are therefore free to inject words and phrases, utter clarifying remarks, make gestures, or even help the teller along with his tale if appropriate. These interactions are very subtle and in no way interfere with the performance of a good tale. Likewise, no good tale can be told without the responses of an active audience, and no good tale can be told without the traditional "warming" period to create the right atmosphere. Like the prayers and sermons, the tales are usually preceded—if there is an audience present to act as respondents—by songs, spiritual or otherwise, and then by games, riddles, jokes, and dozens. As previously mentioned, the friendly teasing relaxes the audience and serves the same purpose as the *akuko eji awake nti* in Igbo: it prepares the group so that it will participate in the event by responding to certain cues given by the teller.

The teller's call and the audience's reply are often simultaneous. Clearly they must be distinguished on the printed page, and separating them formally as is done here helps clarify the degree to which the speaker and the audience rely on back-and-forth interplay to develop and perpetuate a rhythmic flow once the tale begins.[24]

The following notational conventions have been used to provide more information concerning the context in which these tales were told. Double exclamation marks indicate loudness, and triple exclamation marks, extreme loudness. Parentheses enclose indications of non-verbal communicative behaviors, such as long pauses, laughter, eye or hand movements, or meditations. Dashes indicate interruptions or pauses in thought or speech. Ellipsis dots show omissions. A series of hyphens indicates phonological lengthening, as in O-o-o-kay! Italics are used for responses and for emphasis on words or phrases. Square brackets enclose translations or interpolations of words or letters.

These tales were told around a fire site at a local store just after nightfall on Wadmalaw Island. Approximately twenty or thirty people gathered, eating crabs and roasting hot dogs while they waited for the storytelling session to begin. The order here does not necessarily reflect the order in which tales were told. Further, some tellers were better performers than others and thus were asked to tell several tales before the session ended.


"The Man and the Skita [Mosquito]" is an extension of the Clever Slave Motif J1114.01 (more commonly known in the United States as an "old marster and John" tale) and Motif H961, Task Performed by Cleverness. It falls vaguely within Tale Type 920 III, Impossible Task.[25] In this tale the philosophical outlook of Ber Rabbit prevails: even when faced with almost insurmountable odds, one can survive not through physical strength but through one's own wit and intelligence.

## The Man and the Skita [Mosquito]

Mr. James Frazier

One upon a time, way back in the olden day—some part of
Alabama—way down South.    *Yeah!*    Black man had done a
crime.    *Um huh!*    And they put em in prison    *Um huh!*
—And those days they was punish you the way they feel
like.    *Yeah! Uh huh! That's right!*

So they put this man in a rice field, which was very low in
the time a summer time.    *Uh huh! Summer time*    And mosquito
was very bad.    *Um hum. Very bad*    And he told this man, say,
"The only way you'll free, if you go in and plow, and don't
knock no mosquito. Don't, Don't—Don't raise a hand at
mosquito. Let skita bite."    *Um hum, let skita bite! Yeah! Don't
knock em!*

So, this young man went on and plow and plow and plow,
and the skita de bite em so much, he stop—and talk to his
master, bossman, or whatever he was.    *Uh hum! Yeah, stop and
talk!*

Say—"Ah, Master, look a here!! I see a pasture full of cow
(peering into the distance). That cow yonder (points) with the
(slapping his shoulder) the white here, (slapping his back as if to
kill a mosquito), the black here (hitting leg), the brown here. That
cow de yours?"    *(Listeners laughing uproariously)*

Say (laughing), "Yeah! That cow de mine."    *(Listeners
laughing) Killing skita now!*

Yeah, killin the skita.

So he plow on, plow on, skita bite em again!!!    *Um huh
(still laughing)*    So he call he master again. Say,
"Master?"    *Uh huh! Master?*    I see another cow with white
here (again slapping his face as if killing mosquitoes), black here
(slapping his arm), brown here (slapping his back). That cow de
yours?"    *Yeah!*

Man say, "Yeah, that cow de mine."    *Um huh (much
laughter and clapping)*

And e keep on saying that until the days is done.    *Um huh!
Yeah! Donem!*    After the days is done!    *Um huh*    Well, the

skita was done!    *Um hum. Yeah! Skita been done!*    And that
was that one!!!    *(Clapping) Yeah! (laughter) Kill em! Yes sir!*
 O-o-o-kay! Another good one! O-o-o-kay, the next one. Tell
another one!    *(Laughter and clapping)*


"Ber Rabbit in the Peanut Patch" is classified as Type 1310 A, Motif
581.2, Briar-Patch Punishment for Rabbit. This tale is often the sequel
to "The Tar Baby" (Tale Type 175), a tale still told and retold on the
Sea Islands by young and old. The fact that the audience already knew
this tale well only added to the excitement of the occasion. The teller's
creativity was displayed by the variations in his facial expressions and
the energy and enthusiasm with which he chose to tell his tale. A well-
known and favorite storyteller, this man never disappointed his audience. He spoke very rapidly and thus did not wait for a response to
every word or phrase.


## Ber Rabbit in the Peanut Patch

Mr. Ted Williams

 Ah—Anybody else? Anybody else?    *You go ahead and
talk!*    I go—I gone tell a—a few short story.    *Uh humm. Tell
em!*    About the rabbit and the—and the man.    *Um humm. Ber
Rabbit! Ber Rabbit!*
 The man catch the rabbit in his um—in peanuts patch.
Trap em in he peanuts patch.
And he say, "Now, Ber Rabbit, you always sharp!
You always go a lot of scheme!
But now, you know what I gone do with you?
I gone punish you.
I gone throw you in that fire!!    *(Laughter from audience)*
 Ber Rabbit, O Lord! (Pausing as if to think)
I tell you what he do.
"I tell you what you do—old man (as if thinking to himself).
Throw me in the fire!" (shrugs his shoulders)    *Throw me in the
fire!*
 The man say, "No, you too free!" (shaking his head).

Say, "I ain't gone do that!
I tell you what I gone do with you.
I gone throw you in that river!"    *The river!*
    Ber Rabbit say, "I tell you what you do.
Throw me in that river!    *Yeah! The river!*    Let me drown there!
Just throw me in the river—let me.
I want a dead anyhow.
Throw me in the river!"    *Um huh!*
    Man say, "No-o-o-. I ain't gone throw you in there cause you
too free! You too sharp!"
And he say (pausing as if to think),
"I know! You know what I gone do with you, Ber
Rabbit?"    *Yeah!*
    (Unconcerned) "What you gone do? What you gone do?"
He carry em to the man briarwood patch. And boy!!!
(shakes his head). That briar ben about that high
(raises his hand above his head).
    Say, "Ber Rabbit, I gone throw you in that briarwood patch."
    (Moaning) "OOO-o-o-o Lord!!!    *(Much laughter)*
(Wrinkling his nose and crooking his hand and fingers)
    Ple-e-e-ase do-o-o-n't throw me in there!!!    *(Much laughter
from the imitation)*
    *(Whining and shaking)* Dem briarwood stick me
up!    *(Laughter)*
Ple-e-e-ase" (whimpering).
    And he take Ber Rabbit, say, "Oh! I got you now, Ber
Rabbit!"
    "OOO-o-o-o, don't throw me in there!    *Got em!*
I rather you kill me!" (holding hands as if praying).
    So, e take the rabbit and thow em in briarwood patch.
    The rabbit say, "You fool you! This where I born and
raise!"    *(Much laughter and clapping among the audience).
Born and raise!*
    That's all now! I ain't coming back in!    *Born and raise!*
*(Laughter)*


"The Buzzard and the Hawk" is only one of many, many tales told of
Ber Buzzard and his unsavory eating habits; yet the buzzard is revered

on the Sea Islands for his patience and faith in the Lord's salvation. The buzzard is not an animal that the islanders are ambivalent about. He keeps his distance and they keep theirs; they never kill him for sport but actually depend on him to help them locate dead dogs and farm animals which may have strayed away and got lost in the marsh. Variants of "The Buzzard and the Hawk" are numerous and can be found in just about any collection of African-American tales.[26]

Before beginning this tale the speaker had told a series of well-received stories. He paused at the outset to tease the audience into asking for more.

## The Buzzard and the Hawk

Mr. Ted Williams

Y'all know—(pauses and addresses the audience)—I ain't taking too much time?   *No! Uh uh!!*

Huh?   *No!*

Y'all know about the buzzard?   *Uh uh*

(Looking at the audience as if puzzled) Y'all didn't hear about the buzzard?   *No! (laughing)*

(Again, acting even more surprised) Y'all ain't heard about the buzzard?!!!   *(The audience laughs at his expression) Tell us!! Tell us about the buzzard?*

The buzzard and the monkey!   *(laughing and clapping)*

*Tell us about the buzzard and the monkey! (more laughing and clapping)*

Louis Jerden, Louie Jerden tell y'all about that now, y'all! (Looks at the older members of the audience.) The old people know about Louie Jerden and the buzzard!   *(Elderly members nod and smile knowingly)*

You know the buzzard always was a—a nice educated animal, you know!   *(Nods) Um hum! um hum!*

E take e time—(reflecting) just like he done with the hawk.   *(Nods and um hums in unison)*

Him and the hawk was sitting down on the limb one day, and he said—Him and the hawk had a consolation [consultation].

Say, "I'm very hungry!!!"

The hawk say, "I'm hungry too! (rubbing his stomach). Lord—O
Lord! My stomach! I too hungry!"
The buzzard say (patiently), "Wait on the Lord—"
And e look up—Nothing for dead—NOTHING, you know
So the buzzard say (exasperated), "MAN!!!"
    The hawk say, "I can't wait no longer!"
    So when he look (straightens his back as if seeing something
interesting), a little sparrow come along. And—and—and the
hawk get up and run at the sparrow and hit a tree    *Uh huh!*
    And the buzzard sit on he limb and look the hawk, look at the
hawk, when he run into tree. The buzzard say (nodding his head
knowingly and pointing his finger), "I tell you wait on the Lord.
Now I gone eat you now!"    *(Much laughter and jovial
responding among the audience)*


Though the buzzard is revered for his patience and intelligence, he is
not, according to the islanders, as "smaat" in any way as the monkey.
"The Buzzard and the Monkey" is an example of the syncretism of
folk culture and pop culture. Louis Jordan, a prominent rhythm and
blues artist, recorded the popular tune "Straighten Up and Fly Right"
in the 1940s, basing the song on the situation portrayed in this folktale.
Here one sees a direct reborrowing of the pop recording back into the
folk tradition. The teller depends on his listeners' familiarity with the
tale and the song to elicit their support in singing the chorus from the
record. In this manner he transforms the old tale into a cante fable, or
"singing tale."[27]


## The Buzzard and the Monkey

Mr. Ted Williams

    —So the buzzard done the same ting with the monkey! The
buzzard got so-o-o-o-o hungry one day, he couldn't hold it
(holding his stomach). So he went to the monkey.
(Aside to one of the listeners) Him and the monk was good
friend, you know.    *(Listener nods) Um hum!*
    He say (loudly), "Brother Monk!!!"

(Aside)—eh—everybody tink monkey just like color, black man, you know. Could fool em!    *(Unison) Yeah!*    But e couldn't fool that monkey!! (shaking his head).

Ah—"Look here!!! Let's go—you want a go for a ride?"

E say, "Yeah!" Say, "Ah—I don't mind going for a ride. But you (scratching his head and hesitating), I can't fly. You know? I ain't got no wing. I can swing (swings his arm). But, I can't fly!"

E say, "Well (hesitates as if thinking about the monkey's situation). Now come on! I'll—I'll, I'll—I got the wing. I'll fly you!"

So the buzzard—the monkey jump on the buzzard back, sort of circle around and show em view, you know. (Looking up in the sky) And buzzard start de lie. Start de show em old man John farm—rice pond. Say, "See all that rice pond there?" (pointing downward).

"Yeah!"

"De mine!" He duck around (makes a rapid downward gesture with his wrist and arm). Monkey de hold!    *(Laughter)*

"All that tata over there?"

"Yeah!"

"De mine!"    *Yeah! De mine!*

"Yeah!"

Monkey de hold right on!

So e say, "Well, let's go a little higher, let's catch some breeze, brother monkey."

Buzzard shoot up! (makes a rapid swing with his hand and arm). Monkey de hold!    *Yeah! (laughter)*

And e go up a little higher, e start de show em different ting. And show de the sun and moon.

Say, "See all them yonder?    *Uh huh!*
You know I got de fight over them."    *Yeah, fight over em!*

So e start—e say (in a whisper), "Well, getting hungry now—I go duck and throw monkey down, see?"    *Yeah! Throw em down*

So e got a little higher! (raises his hand). Higher!! (raises hand and arm even higher). Higher!!! (raises arm straight up in the air). And e start de duck, and de monkey start de choke em.    *De choke em!*

Say, "Ah—Monkey?"

"Ah? I ain't doing nothing!"

Monkey say, "Well-let-start-for-straighten-up-and-fly-a-little-right-now. Yougettingalittledamnhighupinair—hear!!"    *(Much laughter and cheering from the listeners)*

(Laughs) So e gone little higher (points upward). E choke em and e say, Ah! The, the monkey tell the buzzard. E say (confused), the buzzard tell the monkey, "Say, Monkey? Release your holt and I set you for free!!"    *Yeah, release em!*

And the monkey say, "Well, got dang, let me tell you one ting now!! You tell me, say, you gone show me the view and do this and do that! Now you WAY UP HERE! I want you de straighten up and fly right!"

Tell em, say, buzzard tell, say, "Well—well—ah! Release your holt and I'll set you free!!!    *(Cheers from the audience)*

So (laughs) Louie Jerdon write that record, you know!! Right now, we can sing that!    *Yeah! Yeah!*
(Stands and walks around the crowd) Straighten up and fly right! (Asks members of the audience) Who understand what I'm say now?    *(The audience joins in singing)*
Straighten up and fly right!
Straighten up and fly right!
Do long, papa, don't you blow your trump!

(Laughs) Ha! Ha! Aint that what e say?!!!    *Yeah! (Much laughter and cheering)*

---

"Peter and the Rock" is classified as Type 774, Jest about Christ and Peter. It is only one of a series of tales told on the islands about how Peter is made to look ridiculous because of his greed or some other sinful trait.

This speaker adjusted his narrative style to a rather formalized language to tell a somewhat religious tale. As his tale progressed, his language became increasingly creolized and his audience showed a greater involvement with the content of the tale. Near the end, the speaker seemed more concerned with delighting the audience than with his language: his manner became more relaxed; he put more of himself into the tale; and the audience responded with tremendous enthusiasm. At the end his language reverted to the rather formal style ("That's it, now!").

## Peter and the Rock

Mr. Ted Williams

I going in the Bible now.    *Okay. Okay. All right now.*
Now—he—you, everybody know the, the Scripture?    *Yeah, Yeah!*
Ah—Peter—James, John, and—Christ all, all of em?    *Yeah*
And, well, you know, Christ—always on a good mission. He always was doing good thing for people, you know, in his, eh, demonstration.    *In demonstration. Yeah!*

So—ah—come a time when—when—when Christ want a—go to—from Jericho to Jerusalem.    *Uh huh*
And he come out de his twelve disciple and ask them.
Say—"Now I want you, two disciple de go with me.
I want two *good* disciple for go with me."    *Yeah, two* good *disciple for go!*

So you know Christ always want John de go with em.    *Uh hum, want John de go*
Then Peter come—you know Peter was always was *slick.* Peter say, "Well, I go with you too."    *Yeah! (laughing) go with you too.*

So when they go on the road de going de, ah, Jerusalem from Jericho, then Christ say, "Ahm, *everybody* pick up a rock! We want de demostrate the cross.
We want de tote a rock from here—from Jerusalem to Jericho— from Jericho de Jerusalem."    *Jericho de Jerusalem*

So, Christ got a rock—
John got a BIG rock—
and then Peter got a li-i-i-sma-a-a-ll rock about the size of this

instrument here (holding up the microphone).    *Um hum*
*(whispers)*
That de Peter all right now.    *(Quiet laughter)*

So (laughs), when he got al-l-l-most de Jerusalem, Christ say,
"Everybody lay he rock down, and let e rest off a little bit a for e
get in the city."

So Peter say, "Well, thank God!
Y'all tote that big rock, but I got this little one here.
I ain't tired!"    *(Laughter from the audience)*
And de set the rock down—and rest and sleep.

So, when they wake up—then Christ say,
"Okay! I know y'all disciple hungry now."
Say, "I gone turn this rock in de bread."    *Bread!*
So dey turn in John rock de bread.    *Turn em de bread!*
John had a BIG rock—turn em de bread.    *Um humm.*
So John had a BIG piece of rock, bread.
They turn e rock in de bread.
He had a big rock.    *Big bread!*

Uh huh.
So Peter ben so chafe [vexed],
Peter turn e—he turn he Peter rock de bread, but Peter just had a
li-i-i-piece of rock.    *(Much laughter)*
Was a little read—(laughing) bread.
So—ah—and so when de ready,    *(laughter)*
When they de finish
Done—eat—and start for walk off—

"So, okay! Let me—everybody get a rock now. See the city right
over there. Everybody get another rock."

So John get a small rock this time.    *Um hum, a small one!*
Christ get a small one.
Peter get a BIG old rock.    *Big one this time! (Much laughter)*

And they get in Jerusalem, Christ say, "Everybody put e rock
down."
And Christ walk up and look at the big beautiful city.

And Christ step up and say,
"On this rock I build my church!"    *Uh hum!*

And Peter say, "OOO! Hell no!!!"    *(Much laughter, cheering,
and clapping from the audience)*
"You bina make (laughing),
you bina—you bina make bread all the time on the other rock!!"
Tell em, "You gone make bread now cause I got a BIG rock!
You gone make bread with this rock!!!"    *(Much clapping and
urging from the listeners to tell another tale)*

That's it now—I got some more, but I'll tell y'all later!

## Three Gullah Tales with African Parallels

Hear tell say Ber Rabbit ben come here from Africa.

The Gullah tales with African parallels that are included here
are only a minute sampling of tales on the Sea Islands having roots in
African literary traditions. The student of comparative literature can
discover topics for extensive comparisons from the collections of Joel
Chandler Harris, Elsie Clews Parsons, Ruth Finnegan, Florence Cronise and Henry Ward, and Richard Dorson, among others.[28] These
topics manifest themselves through themes, plots, characterizations,
and other conventions, all worthy of detailed exploration in themselves
but by far exceeding the limitations of this book.

I took certain precautionary measures in collecting the African
tales to try to eliminate the possibility of receiving tales that might have
origins other than African.[29] I made no requests, however, for particular types or kinds of tales: the stories recorded on each continent were
collected at random on any subject that the informants chose.

The African tales in this book came from Uzoaba, an Igbo village
near Owerri, Nigeria.[30] The Igbo culture was selected for study and
comparison with Gullah because the linguistic features seemingly most
prominent on Wadmalaw Island, South Carolina (the island on which I
have conducted most of my research), are traceable to the Igbo lan-

guage. For example, the pronominal system in contemporary Gullah
still reveals such features as the singular and plural second-person pronouns *unu* and *hunu,* respectively. These features correspond to the
pronoun *una,* the second-person plural marker in contemporary Igbo.
Likewise, one pronoun still expresses the range of third-person pronoun possibilities in Gullah for many speakers. Although Igbo does
employ two pronouns—/o/, the vowel sound in *doe,* and /ọ/, the
sound of *aw* as in *law* the two systems are similar in that the same
pronoun may be used to refer to both male and female. While it is true
that many West African languages do follow this undifferentiating
practice, other linguistic features link the lexicon of Gullah and Igbo,
including [də], the locative, and the form of the verb *to be.* (This
subject is considered in greater detail in Chapter 4.)

In addition to linguistic features, there are similarities between the
two cultures in hair-wrapping techniques, food preparation, child-rear-
ing practices, and other social customs already discussed, enough similarities to suggest a concentration of Igbo ancestral background for
residents of Wadmalaw and perhaps other islands as well. It is well
known among the islanders that each island carries its unique pattern of
language and culture, and these patterns may perhaps indicate carry-
overs from elsewhere in West Africa.

As Cronise and Ward have observed, some African tales have parallels in cultures in which there is only the remotest possibility of mu-
tual influence. The tale of the "Tar Baby," for example, is found in
various versions in most folklore. Certain themes may indeed be universal, just as some linguistic features are universal. The similarities
between the Igbo and Sea Island tales cannot be dismissed as coinci-
dental, however, because the genetic link between the African and the
African-American people provides the basis for cultural and literary
continuity.[31]

The evidence of literary continuity is most apparent in the handling
of traditional themes and characters. Both cultures delight in imbuing
physically insignificant and seemingly helpless creatures with extraor-
dinary mental acumen. Their superior intelligence and discretion make
these small beings not only godlike in powers but models for much
stronger creatures to emulate. The "helpless" animal may take the
form of the spider of the Gold Coast, the turtle of the Slave Coast, the
rabbit of the Sierra Leone region, or the *hlakanyana* of South Africa.

Mortars made from palm trees are traditionally used to pound rice and corn. Similar mortars are still used throughout Africa

Regardless of the region, these animals are heroic figures in the same tradition as Ber Rabbit in Gullah and inland black literature, or Ananse the spider in Caribbean literature.

In attempting to explain why a weak creature like a rabbit was selected as a folktale hero in black America, traditional theories have posited the powerless being as the personification of the slave, who had to be extraordinarily clever to avoid and survive the wrath of the slave master. While this concept is theoretically sound and indeed operative, it loses validity in light of the evidence that physically insignificant creatures were revered for their intelligence in Africa long before the African-American was ever subjected to the cruelties of slavery. Seldom does one find massive or ferocious animals like the lion, the leopard, the elephant, or the hippopotamus depicted in African literature as shrewd and insightful. They are continuously portrayed as stupid and as perpetually duped and humiliated by smaller animals who must from necessity live by their wits, not by their strength. This concept of shrewdness and cunning embodied within a tiny animal is apparent, for example, in "The Spider, the Elephant and the Hippopotamus," a tale told to Finnegan by the Limba and also told to Cronise and Ward by the Temne speakers.[32] In this tale the spider uses his wit against the power of two larger animals. We can find a parallel in Harris's Sea Island tale "Mr. Terrapin and Mr. Bear." Likewise, an Igbo tale of Nnabe, the tortoise, making a riding horse out of an alligator and insulting him midstream finds a parallel in Parsons's Ber Rabbit making a riding horse out of Ber Alligator on the Sea Islands. This same tale has a parallel in the Caribbean, with Ananse, the spider, riding the tiger's back.[33] In another Igbo tale "Nnabe and the Fruits" (given here with its Sea Island companion tale), Nnabe is able to defraud a whole host of animals; there are similarities in the way Ber Rabbit outwits Ber Wolf in "Ber Rabbit, Ber Wolf, and the Butter."

The spider, tortoise, and hare are shown to be inferior to and answerable only to a higher immortal being, Chineke in Igbo and the Lord in Sea Island tales. Here, for example, Nnabe and Ber Rabbit seek more knowledge from their creator in "Nnabe and Chineke" and "Ber Rabbit and the Lord." While both animals are revered for their wit and ingenuity, both are kicked out of heaven when they attempt to cheat God. Both continue to bear the scars of God's wrath: Nnabe has a broken shell as a result of his fall, and Ber Rabbit has a white tail as a reminder that God threw a cup of milk at him as he was ejected.

In the animal tales from both continents, the central characters nearly always function as though they were human beings. That they are lower animals personifying humans is secondary to the intent and purpose of the tales. The animals' roles are seldom comic in the style of American cartoon characters like Mickey Mouse, Donald Duck, or Bugs Bunny. Tales of Nnabe and Ber Rabbit are designed to represent mature individuals reacting in adult situations of daily life. In tale after tale, the listeners are confronted with multifaceted personalities which they sometimes like, sometimes dislike. There are differences: Nnabe is far more vicious in his interactions, for example, than Ber Rabbit. In many tales he is consciously cruel and tyrannical. Ber Rabbit, on the other hand, is seldom depicted as self-seeking. He is known as a trickster, or one "smart too much," but he generally resorts to chicanery only to preserve his life.

While many favorite African and African-American tales involve animals acting like human beings, many tales are told of mermaids (*mama water* or *daddy water*), great hunters, chiefs, and the common person in struggles against the forces of nature. A frequent theme among the Igbo, Ibebio, and Yoruba involves crimes against the family: a member of one's family kills another member, and the ill deed is revealed by the murdered person's bones. Similar tales are also told on the Sea Islands. Here "The Three Pear[s], or the Singing Bones" is compared with "The Flower, or the Singing Bones." Tales of this type are customarily accompanied by lyrics, which the audience usually participates in singing. These tales involve the audience fully and are usually welcome diversions from the traditional trickster exploits.

The Gullah and Igbo tales that follow demonstrate the similarities in plot and character that have been mentioned. Most of the African informants had little or no familiarity with the English language. Each tale was told in a familiar setting in the speaker's native tongue and then translated into English with the aid of a bilingual consultant from the village. The Gullah tales have been edited to eliminate stuttering, false starts, and constructions which are not confusing in speech but which, because they are distractions, would most likely make the text more difficult to understand, and ultimately would cause the similarities between the plots to seem more obscure. Features such as the formulaic or introductory verb *say* and the preverbal markers *de, ben, bina,* and *don* have been retained to aid in perpetuating the original flavor of the tales. (See Appendix I for a transcription of one story into

Hairwrapping is an ancient African tradition that survives on the islands.

an older Gullah spelling and syntax.) As I have emphasized, however, no transcription can fully capture the aura of the nonverbal interplay which is a dynamic aspect of any oral tradition.

1. "Ber Rabbit and the Lord" and its Igbo parallel, "Nnabe and Chineke [The Tortoise and the Lord]," are classified as Type 2 tales, which are concerned with how the various animals received their physical characteristics. "Ber Rabbit and the Lord" is classified as Motif A2231.1, Animal Characteristics: Punishment for Discourteous Answer to God. "Nnabe and Chineke" is Motif A2231.1.4, Discourteous Answer: Tortoise's Shell. These are two of the few tales where Ber Rabbit and Nnabe are actually punished for their mischievous deeds. It is important to note, however, that their punishment is meted out not by mortals like themselves but by a supreme being.

## Ber Rabbit and the Lord

Mr. Jonas Mickell
Wadmalaw Island, South Carolina

Once upon a time Ber Rabbit went de the Lord for get more knowledge, more wisdom. And the Lord tell Ber Rabbit, "All right! I want you de bring anything white de me. Anything white."

Rabbit went out in the field, and he went out meet [happened to meet] Ber Partridge there. [Ber Rabbit] had a bag, and [he] tell Ber Partridge: "I betcha all you, all couldn't full this bag [I bet you aren't big enough to fill up this bag]."

Partridge say, "How you mean?"

[Ber Rabbit told Ber Partridge], "Run in here, see if you can full this bag."

All the partridge full up [spread his wings], run in, full the bag. Ber Rabbit put that on he shoulder and carry em de the Lord. [The Lord said], "All right!" [But the Lord] gone send em back. Ber Rabbit, he send em back.

"Well, I want you now, Ber Rabbit, de bring me a

rattlesnake!" Danger!!! [The Lord was going to] put Ber Rabbit
where all the danger [was]!

Ber Rabbit tell em, "All right!"

Ber Rabbit gone out in field and find a rattlesnake, and he
have a cane and tell Ber Rattlesnake: "Ber Snake, you ain't long
as this cane!" Ber Rattlesnake run alongside the cane.

Ber Rabbit say, "No! I don't mean that way. I want you
run in!"

Ber Snake run in—rattlesnake run in Ber cane. Tshhht, Ber
Rabbit stop this hole up, carry em de the Lord.

He say, "Now, all right now, Ber Rabbit, you put in five [you
did well]! You good! You good enough! Now I want you, Ber
Rabbit, I want you de bring a gator tail de me—from the water."

Rabbit say, "I can bring that!"

Rabbit drank up heself [got up his nerve], and he gone down
de the river, and he tell Ber Gator, say, "Ber Gator???"

Ber Gator say, "Ber Rabbit, where you going?"

De say, "I going over here to Adale—and ain't no way I can
get there. Ain't got no boat."

Ber Gator tell Ber Rabbit, say, "Jump on my head. I'll carry
you over there."

Ber Rabbit jump on Ber Gator head. When Ber Gator get
cross to other shore, Ber Rabbit knock the Ber Gator in e head
and knock all he teeth out, and carry em to the Lord. All right!

Ber Lord [Rabbit] say, "All right, Ber Rabbit [Lord], what
you want de do again?"

[Ber Lord] say, "I want you de bring me some cow milk."

Rabbit say, "All right!"

Rabbit bex [vex] the cow and the cow run around, run
around, run around and twirl around, around, around, he feet.
Rabbit snatch em! The cow fall down! The Rabbit got em up
between the leg and milk that and carry milk to Ber Lord.

"All right," Ber Rabbit say, "Now Lord!"

[The Lord said], "I want you de bring me some bull milk."

"All right!"

Ber Rabbit jump down there de bex, de get out the bull, de
bex the bull. Say, "Bull, you can't do the same ting [as the
cow]." Say, "I want you to run around this tree."

The bull run around this tree and the bull fall down! The rabbit get between the bull de start to pull them two leg.

He gone back de the Lord and he call, "Lord—e got e milk."

[But the Lord] tell Ber Rabbit, say, "where the hell you see a bull give milk?"

The same milk what he carry, de the cow milk, the Lord take that milk and sling em behind Ber Rabbit tail, cause em de [become] white. And tell Ber Rabbit, "Go head, [rabbit] and dog will be condition [enemies forever]. If the bush crack you got to go!!!"

## Nnabe and Chineke [The Tortoise and the Lord]

Song story sung in Igbo by Samuel Onunwa,
Bartholomew Amaugo, Kevin Chiedusie,
and Francis Mbah
Translated into English by Victor C. Ihejetoh

Chakpii?  *Haa!!!*
Once upon a time  *And a time*
   *there came!*
As God was going  *Amanye**
And the tortoise was
   returning  *Amanye*
They met on the way  *Amanye*
The tortoise ask God for
   wisdom  *Amanye*
God dug his hands into his
   pocket  *Amanye*
And pulled out a hard
   rock  *Amanye*
And gave it to the tortoise to
   break  *Amanye*
To break its kola shell  *Amanye*
The tortoise took it  *Amanye*

And tried to break the
   shell  *Amanye*
In the process  *Amanye*
He wounded his
   hand  *Amanye*
The tortoise went to the
   fence  *Amanye*
And dug some soil  *Amanye*
And said, "My dear Father
   God  *Amanye*
Please grow for me  *Amanye*
The soil of wisdom  *Amanye*
In my head"  *Amanye*
God shouted  *Amanye*
"Oko-ko-ko-ko  *Amanye*
My son tortoise  *Amanye*
Who told you  *Amanye*

*[an agreement chant like *Amen* or *Right on*]

That that such could
  be?"   *Amanye*
God then went   *Amanye*
And counted twenty
  coins   *Amanye*
And gave them to the
  tortoise   *Amanye*
To go get some wine   *Amanye*
"But don't buy palm tree
  wine   *Amanye*
Nor that of the palm
  wine   *Amanye*
Don't bring it in *udu* [a kind of
  bowl]   *Amanye*
Nor with *ebele* [Igbo native
  pot]"   *Amanye*
The tortoise went   *Amanye*
And thought for a year   *Amanye*
He collected plantain
  leaves   *Amanye*
And those of banana   *Amanye*
He extracted and
  extracted   *Amanye*
Until he filled the
  mortar   *Amanye*
And carried it to God   *Amanye*
"My Father God   *Amanye*
Please have the wine   *Amanye*
Don't drink with the
  mouth   *Amanye*
Don't drink with the
  head   *Amanye*
Nor any other source"   *Amanye*
God agreed   *Amanye*
He thought and
  thought   *Amanye*
And thought for a year   *Amanye*
He made an incision in his
  leg   *Amanye*

And poured in some
  wine   *Amanye*
An incision in his
  hand   *Amanye*
Poured in some wine   *Amanye*
Collected the cock   *Amanye*
And gave it to the
  tortoise   *Amanye*
In a year's time   *Amanye*
God told him   *Amanye*
To bring a mother and
  child   *Amanye*
At the end of the
  year   *Amanye*
God met the tortoise   *Amanye*
"My son tortoise   *Amanye*
Where is mother and
  child?"   *Amanye*
The tortoise said   *Amanye*
Mother went to war   *Amanye*
The father is with
  child   *Amanye*
God shouted   *Amanye*
"Oko-ko-ko-ko   *Amanye*
My son tortoise   *Amanye*
Who ever told you   *Amanye*
The mother goes to
  war   *Amanye*
The father could have a
  child?"   *Amanye*
For his impertinence   *Amanye*
God pushed him down from
  heaven   *Amanye*
And that is why   *Amanye*
The tortoise has a cracked
  shell   *Amanye*
Haa!   *Amanye*
Haa!   *Amanye*
Chakpii!!   *Haa!!*

2. "Ber Rabbit, Ber Wolf, and the Butter" is Animal Type 15, The Theft of Butter by Playing Godfather, and Deception Motif K401.1, Dupe's Food Eaten and Then Blame Fastened on Him. Some previous commentators have made references to a fire-jumping scene in other versions of this Sea Island tale.[34] The African parallel for this tale, "Nnabe and the Fruits" does involve a jumping scene, where Nnabe is expected to jump to his death (Motif K891). However, being the sly, perceptive little animal that he is, Nnabe has made prior arrangements for his getaway once he completes his jump.

## Ber Rabbit, Ber Wolf, and the Butter

James Oree
Wadmalaw Island, South Carolina

Ber Wolf de tell Ber Rabbit, "Let's make some butter, okay?"

So Ber Rabbit and Ber Wolf, they got together. They decided to make some butter. Now, they both was married. And between the rabbit and the wolf, the rabbit thought he had a little more sense than the wolf. Okay?

*Um hum! Yeah!*

So what happen, the rabbit and the wolf, they decided de make the butter.

By and by Ber Rabbit tell the wolf that his wife was expecting a baby. And that he had de go check on the baby! Every now and then he had de go and check on the baby!

So they work in the field. They went in the field and they start de work. They was hoeing, de working they crop. They planted it together—you know, do everything together. They planted they crop. And rabbit said to the wolf, "Ber Wolf? Look a here, Ber Wolf!" Say, "My wife de call me! Say, I—Shah [a typical Sea Island exclamation]! I have for go check on my wife now. Shah!—My wife de expecting a baby, and—"

[Ber Wolf] say, "Okay! Okay, Ber Rabbit, go head."

When he come back, [Ber Wolf] say, "Did your wife had the baby?"

[Ber Rabbit] say, "Yeah!"

[Ber Wolf] say, "What the baby is?"

[Ber Rabbit] say, "De baby girl de name Start Em!"

(Aside) See, he was start de eat the butter then, you see? He was begin de eat the butter—what they made.

They work for a little while—on they went on. [Then Ber Rabbit] say, "HUSH—Shh—Sha—Tsk—My wife de call me again, Man!" Ha! Say, "I got de—I hear something." (listens). [Ber Wolf] say, "What's that, Ber Rabbit?" (looks around with hand to his ear).

"My wife call me. My wife expect that baby, that baby girl coming." Wolf say, "Well, spect you better go see about em again, Ber Rabbit—see about em again."

So Ber Rabbit gone and eat most half the butter and come back de the field. Say he ben see about he wife. [Ber Wolf] say, "What baby girl name, Ber Rabbit?" [Ber Rabbit] gives her name Half Em! Ha! Most Half Em!—okay? Most half em! (laughing to himself).

(Aside still laughing) But he was almost halfway in de butter—eating the butter.

Afterward now [after Ber Rabbit again pretended to check on his wife] then he finish eat the butter [and he said, "The name of] the last one is Donem." And then the wolf, when 12:00 o'clock come that day, say, "Well, Ber Rabbit, let's go up and check on our package, on our butter that we has."

*Yeah!*

Ber Rabbit go in [They] look in the refrig— "Oh, Oh, Oh, Oh, Ber Rabbit!!!" [Ber Wolf] say, "You ate all the butter!" Say, "That what you was doing here!"

Ber Rabbit say, "No! Not me!!" Say, "I didn't ate no butter!" And say, "Now—" (shaking his head).

Ber Wolf say, "Yeah, because I was in the field working." Say, "Now all the time you kept coming, off and on—You KNOW you de eating the butter."

And then the rabbit said, "Ber Wolf?" He say, "If you tink I de ate the butter," say, "Why don't you let us go in the sun—let us go in the sun.

*Right! Right!*

And then we'll know which one eat the butter. We'll go and lie in the sun and the sun de melt the butter out of the one de eat em."

So they went for lay in the sun. So by and by Ber Wolf fell sleep. Okay?

*Yeah!*

And after the wolf fell sleep, then the butter that de melt out Ber Rabbit, he smear all over Ber Wolf. When the wolf wake up he tell Ber Rabbit, say, "If I didn't eat the butter, Rabbit, who ate the butter?"

"You ate the butter, Ber Wolf! Because de all de come out of you!"

The wolf didn't had sense enough to know that he didn't ate the butter. You see? The rabbit cheated him (laughs). You see what happened. The rabbit outsmart the wolf!

## Nnabe and the Fruits

Told in Igbo by Raphael Amaugo
Translated into English by Chinere Ihejetoh

Chakpii!!    *Haa!!*

Once upon a time,    *And a time came*    all the animals decided to do collective farming on a special day. That day was on a market day called *eke* in Igboland. That morning the town crier, who was called informant, took a bell and went ringing through the city telling everyone where the farm was to be. All the animals came out in answer to the bell call and went to the farm. There they agreed that if any of them cut or hurt himself while working, that one would be permitted to go home. On their way to the farm, they saw some delicious fruits which they agreed that none would pick separately, but all would pick and share when the farming was done. It was agreed!

Now Nnabe the tortoise was up to his usual tricky ways. So while the other animals worked and thought of the fruits, he sneaked away and ate them. On his way back to the farm, he killed a baby antelope and spread some of its blood on his hand and showed it to the other animals saying that he had injured himself, and that he should be permitted to go home. The animals agreed.

On the way home, he stopped and finished all the fruits that may have been remaining. Then he did a loathsome deed! For each of the fruits that he had cut open and eaten he filled with his own feces, covered the insides with the outer parts, and sealed them up again so that nobody would know that they had been touched.

So when it was time for the other animals to go home, they went to pick the fruits. When one of them opened the first fruit and saw that it was filled with feces, they opened the second one and the same thing was in that one, and in the next one, and in the next one. So they began discussing among themselves who could have done such a dreadful deed! Finally, they concluded that only Nnabe the tortoise could have been able to perform this deed. Yet they had no proof, so they decided that they would find out who the culprit was by traditional means used in those days.

So they dug a big hole and all the animals were to come out and jump over the hole one by one, and whoever fell into the hole while jumping over it would be caught as the culprit. The tortoise, realizing that he would be exposed before the other animals, thought of a way to escape. He hired the rabbit to dig an underground path from his house to that hole and asked him to come and collect his fee on the *eke* market day. The rabbit agreed!

The day came on which all the animals were to go and jump. They all went to the hole to jump over. Before each one jumped he sang the following song:

> The watcher—the watcher—the watcher
> Who came here—who came here—who came here
> Eh hi eh hi eh hi eh hi eh hi eh hi
> Your legs—your hands that touched
> Or picked the ripe fruit
> Your legs—your hands that touched
> Or picked the ripe fruit
> Everyone should wait and watch patiently
> Everyone should wait and watch patiently
> If I did pick these fruits let me fall
> Into this hole
> If I did pick these fruits let me fall
> Into this hole.

The lion started first and jumped across. Each of the other animals jumped across until at last it was Nnabe the tortoise's time to jump. He sang the song and jumped, but fell into the pit. In the pit he denied that he had eaten the fruit. He said that he fell into the pit because he was overdressed and too heavy to jump. Reluctantly, the other animals agreed that maybe his shell was too heavy and that he should be given another chance to clear himself. So they pulled him out from the pit and let him put off his shell. When he finished, he sang the song again and jumped, but still he fell into the pit. This second time all the other animals were convinced that he was the culprit. For his punishment, he was buried alive in the pit and covered with dirt. However, the tortoise was indeed wise, for he had already had the rabbit dig a path from the pit to his house. So the tortoise went home quietly, laughing to himself and praising himself for outwitting the other animals.

Then the *eke* market day arrived, when the rabbit was to collect his money from the tortoise. So the rabbit went to the tortoise's house and told him that he came to collect his fee. The tortoise did not know what to do, since he did not have the money. So he set another day for the rabbit, explaining that his mother-in-law had died and that he had spent all his money for her funeral. On the newly agreed date, the rabbit went again to collect his fee, and this time the tortoise had conceived of a plan to kill the rabbit. He boiled a big pot filled with water and waited for the rabbit to come. When the rabbit came, the tortoise tried to grab him by his tail, but the rabbit was too fast, and pulled himself loose except for the outer cover of his tail, which was pulled off in Nnabe's hands. To this day that is why the rabbit's tail is whiter than the rest of his body.

Chakpii!!    *Haa!*

3. "The Three Pear[s], or the Singing Bones" is classified as Type 720, My Mother Slew Me; My Father Ate Me; and Motif E631.1, Speaking Bones of Murdered Person Reveal Murder. This tale was not as commonly told on the Sea Islands as it was among the Igbo of Nigeria. Many, many variations wherein crimes were revealed by the murdered person's bones were collected in Nigeria.

## The Three Pear[s], or the Singing Bones

Miss Deeley
Yonges Island, South Carolina

A woman had two children. And e want for make a pie for she husband before e come home from field. He bina plow. So she tell e children, say, "I de go store for get sugar for make pie." Tell em, say, "Don't eat the three pear I leave on the table. I make a pie out em when I de come back."

When she leave for go get the sugar, the girl child de get hungry. E get hungry too much, man! So e gone and look on the pear—look on the pear—look on em—look on em. Finally, she get the pear and eat em. When the woman come home, look, see the pear ben gone, e ask e children, say, "Who eat the pear I ben leave on table here?"

The boy say, "Sister, Mama, Sister. Sister ben eat em." [Then the woman] ask Sister, say, "Who ben eat the pear, Sister?" Sister say, "Brother, Mama, Brother. Brother ben eat em."

"Brother?"
"Sister, Mama, Sister!"
"Sister?"
"Brother, Mama, Brother!"
They go on—go on—go on.

The woman tell Sister, say, "Sister, go lay head on the chop block out there."

Sister gone and lay e head on the chop block out by the woodpile. By and by, the woman come and pick up the axe and de chop Sister head off and bury em in the onion patch. Chop she leg and bury em in de hen house. Chop she arm, bury em in the barnyard. Li [little] bird ben see where e bury em.

When de evening, the daddy come home and ask he wife, say, "Where Sister?" Woman say, "She over the other side de stay with the grandma awhile." By and by, the daddy ben go over de other side for get Sister. The grandma say, "ain't see em." So they de look, de look—and de look for Sister. The woman tell em, say, "Sister run away."

By and by, spring de come and time come for plant onion

again. Woman grow em, get fine mess of em. One evening, they
bina eat supper and woman tell Brother, say, "Go out there in the
onion patch and pull some onion for eat with the peas." So
Brother gone in the onion patch and de start for pull up onion.
But when he de start for pull em, e yeddy [heard] somebody de
sing:

> Brother, Brother, Brother
> Don't pull me hair
> Know mama de kill me
> Bout the three li pear

The boy ben so scare, e gone, run, tell e mother. The woman
didn't believe the child. Tell em, say, "Go out there for get me
some onion, boy!!!"

The boy gone back and try for pull up onion again. He yeddy
somebody de sing and de sing:

> Brother, Brother, Brother
> Don't pull me hair
> Know mama de kill me
> Bout the three li pear

So this time the child de run, de cry, and e de holler. He
daddy ask em, say, "What ben matter de you?" The child tell em
what he de yeddy in de onion patch. So the daddy go for heself
for see what Brother bina talk about. He get de de onion patch,
boot up [stooped down] for pull up onion, and he yeddy Sister de
sing and de sing:

> Daddy, Daddy, Daddy
> Don't you pull me hair
> Know Mama de kill me
> Bout the three li pear

The man ben so bex, he go back in the house and ask he wife
again. Ask em, say, "What ben happen de Sister?" Woman say,
"I ain't know. You know she ben run away—long time now."
The man tell she, say, "Go in onion patch and try for pull up
onion." The woman gone in the onion patch. E boot up, try for
pull up onion. Soon e start for pull, e yeddy Sister de sing and de
sing:

Mama, Mama, Mama
Don't you pull me hair
You know you kill me
Bout the three li pear

The woman ben so scare, e run, run, run til e knock e head
against a tree. Knock em and kill eself.

By and by, the li bird what see em all happen, e sit on the
fence and sing de de daddy where e find Sister bone. Say:

Look in onion patch
Find e li head
Look in barn yard
Find e li leg
Look in hen house
Find e li arm
Po dog suck e bone

The end of that one!

## The Flower, or the Singing Bones

Told in Igbo by Holda Akuchie
Translated into English with the help of Victor C. Ihejetoh

Once upon a time there lived two people born of the same
parents in a village. In Igboland it has long been customary for
one man to have more than one wife. Thus it is important for
bonds of kinship to be shown with the phrase *by the same
mother, same father.* As it was, these two persons had a very rich
father. This rich man went to a bush in the forest and brought a
flower and showed it to his children. He told them that the name
of the flower was *okoko anuii,* meaning "something of joy."
Above all, he told them that whosoever went to that bush would
have half of his wealth and the remaining half would be shared by
the two of them, if they would look for that which is alive and is
not seen.

They entered the forest from different directions in search of
the flower, and while they were looking and looking for it, the

older one told the younger brother not to follow him into the thicker bush in the open forest, for if he should follow him to the forest, he would be killed.

All right?

So the younger one went his own way, and the older one went his own way, both in search of the flower. The younger did not go far in his own direction before he saw the flower and called to the senior brother that he had found it. When the senior brother came to survey the flower, he found it to be the twin of the one the father had shown them. What made the senior brother grow annoyed was not that the younger brother had found the flower but that one who was his junior would be wealthier. So immediately he took the flower from the younger brother and killed him on the spot! Afterwards, he left and went home with the flower and showed it to his mother. The mother was as happy as a queen would be!

The father was away presiding over cases in court because it was very customary for chiefs in those days to preside over village cases. But when the father was told of the accomplishment, he was very happy. The people of the village were also called, and they also shared in the happiness. When the older son was asked the whereabouts of his brother, he told the father that he was still in the forest. So, in the presence of the village people, the older brother was given half of his father's wealth and property. The younger brother was waited for, waited for, and waited for, but he was never seen again.

A day arrived when a hunter was doing some bush hunting in the forest, and saw a bone. He raised up the bone and smelled it. But as he was contemplating the odor, the bone started to sing:

Dinta, dinta, dinta
Dinta, dinta, dinta
Ọkpụkpụ ke ina ele
Ọkpụkpụ ke ina ele
Onye yana nwanne ya kwunu ba nọhia
Ọbụ nwanne gburu mo-o-o-o-o
Ọbụ nwanne gburu mo-o-o-o-o maka flower mo-o-o

Hunter, hunter, hunter
Hunter, hunter, hunter

The bone you are looking at
The bone you are looking at
Is that of him who went
To the bush with his brother
His brother killed him
His brother killed him
For the sake of his flower, oh-oh-oh-oh

The hunter cried and said to himself that it was the son of the
chief who was lost in the bush. The bone sang that particular
song again and again and again. Finally, the hunter took the bone
and carried it back to the village to report what had occurred.
When he reached the chief's house, the bone in the presence of
the mother started to sing again:

Nne, nne, nne
Nne, nne, nne
Ọkpụkpụ ke ina ele
Ọkpụkpụ ke ina ele
Onye yana nwanne ya kwunu ba nọhia
Ọbụ nwanne gburu mo-o-o-o-o
Ọbụ nwanne gburu mo-o-o-o-o maka flower mo-o-o

Mama, Mama, Mama
Mama, Mama, Mama
The bone you are looking at
The bone you are looking at
Is that of him who went
To the bush with his brother
His brother killed him
His brother killed him
For the sake of his flower, oh-oh-oh-oh

The mother cried for her son and sent for the father. When
the father came, the bone started singing again:

Nna, nna, nna
Nna, nna, nna
Ọkpụkpụ ke ina ele
Ọkpụkpụ ke ina ele
Onye yana nwanne ya kwunu ba nọhia

Ọbụ nwanne gburu mo-o-o-o-o
Ọbụ nwanne gburu mo-o-o-o-o maka flower mo-o-o.

Papa, Papa, Papa
Papa, Papa, Papa
The bone you are looking at
The bone you are looking at
Is that of him who went
To the bush with his brother
His brother killed him
His brother killed him
For the sake of his flower, oh-oh-oh-oh

All right?

The great chief called the whole village and asked them to
listen to the bone, which immediately started to sing again and
again and again:

Obodo anyi, obodo anyi, obodo anyi
Obodo anyi, obodo anyi, obodo anyi
Ọkpụkpụ ke ina ele
Ọkpụkpụ ke ina ele
Onye yana nwanne ya kwunu ba nọhia
Ọbụ nwanne gburu mo-o-o-o-o
Ọbụ nwanne gburu mo-o-o-o-o maka flower mo-o-o

My people, my people, my people
My people, my people, my people
The bone you are looking at
The bone you are looking at
Is that of him who went
To the bush with his brother
His brother killed him
His brother killed him
For the sake of his flower, oh-oh-oh-oh

As was customary in those days, the father killed his elder
son in the presence of the people of the village. He grieved sorely
for both his sons for the remainder of his life. This is why it is
not good for a person to do evil, especially in the case of killing
one's brother. The father kept the bone for remembrance, and

whenever he brings out the bone, it sings its sad song. These affairs hurt the mother in her spirit so that she cried at home and away. But after some time had past, the mother again became with child, and gave life to twin boys. They were called by historical names, as is still customary among the Igbo and other African people. They were called Chinedum, "God is my leader" and Onye Gburu Nwanne Ya Ji Uawo, "He who kills the brother is owing."

Chakpii!

*Haa!!*

# 4

---

# The Language

The old-time talk we still de talkem here!
*We still speak Gullah here!*

## History

The factors which nurtured the Sea Island culture also nurtured the development and perpetuation of the unusual Sea Island language called Gullah or Geechee. The geographical isolation, the marginal contact with speakers outside the Sea Island communities, and the social and economic independence contributed to creating an environment where a mixed language could thrive. Gullah is defined as a creole, the language that results when a pidgin, which has no native speakers but comes into existence as the product of communication among speakers of different linguistic backgrounds, takes over as the only language of the community.

The Sea Island language, like the culture, is undergoing transformations. Several varieties of contemporary Gullah can be heard in day-to-day conversation on topics ranging from who is running for president to the best bogging place in the creek. With the exception of the unusual accent, some speakers show little deviation from standard English at all. The degree of standard English acquisition is a reflection of such factors as the level of education, the accessibility or inaccessibility of a given island to outside forces, and the extent of inside social mobility. Just as one hears a form of standard English, one also hears the "real Gullah" spoken by children and adults in all aspects of community life.

The history of Gullah is complicated. It is called a creole language because it is believed to have resulted from the merger of English and languages used along the West African coast, including Ewe, Fante, Efik, Ibebio, Igbo, Yoruba, Twi, Kongo, and Mandinka. Since many African slaves were also brought from the Angola region of West Africa, some researchers suggest that Angola is a possible source for the word *Gullah*; *Geechee* may be derived from the Gidzi, a language and people in the Kissy country of Liberia.[1]

The isolation without a doubt contributed much to the perpetuation of Gullah as the language of the Sea Islands, but it can be credited with achieving even more than that. Growing up as a black majority almost free from outside social influences, such as racial prejudice characteristic of the white-dominated society in the inland parts of the United States, undoubtedly affected the attitudes and perceptions of the islanders, to the extent that few of them wish to leave the islands today. Lorenzo Dow Turner found as late as 1949 that some islanders had never been to the mainland.[2] With improved bridges and roadways, most have easy access to and from the islands; however, several of the elderly informants for this study reported that they had not left their island in at least forty years.

Today, as I have indicated, the islanders are still very private people and will often guard the secrets of their culture just as they make attempts to guard their language. When I asked some Charlestonian informants why they supposed the islanders speak the way they do, they gave this interesting account:

Francis: Why they speak the way they does?

Jean: Why they speak the way they do?

Francis: Oh, I don't know. I think it's [because] they used to use that pump water long ago.[3]

Jean: No-o-o-o. I don't think it has anything to do with the water. I mean, the water do taste different from the city water. But . . .

Francis: I know it's different.

Jean: I really don't think it has anything to do with [the water]. I think it's just, maybe it just the fact that they is isolated more than we are. You know, and . . . ah . . . most people over there just content to be left alone. . . . They don't see many people that . . . ah . . . speak anything different or learn anything different. And they are content with their life, you

Richard Linen reminisces about the past and about how "thing change up now."

know. . . . I really don't know why they speaks that way. I don't . . . I don't guess too many people do know why. . . . But I be knowing it's not the water. It doesn't . . . I mean what goes into your system, it comes out on the other end. I mean that . . . this don't damage the brain, or vocal cord, or anything like that.

Some serious studies of Gullah were undertaken during the first half of the twentieth century, but most of them were linguistically prejudiced. Scholars such as George P. Krapp, Reed Smith, and H. L. Mencken treated the language as a corrupted and intrinsically inferior dialect of English.[4] A. E. Gonzales, a journalist and untrained linguist, provided the most biased and perhaps the most inaccurate linguistic account: "Slovenly and careless of speech, these Gullahs seized upon the peasant English used by some of the early settlers and by the white servants of the wealthier colonist, wrapped their clumsy tongues about it as well as they could, and enriched with certain expressive African words, it issued through their flat noses, and thick lips."[5]

Convictions such as this one were easily refuted by later studies. Lorenzo Turner wrote in 1949: "Up to the present time I have found in the vocabulary of the Negroes in the coastal South Carolina and Georgia approximately four thousand West African words, besides many survivals in syntax, inflections, sounds and intonation. . . . I have recorded in Georgia a few songs the words of which are entirely African."[6] Since Turner's study, most research on Gullah has recognized its legitimacy as a linguistic system. However, no one has studied all of the various categories which are components of any language. As a result of the recent focus on the study of inland black speech in the United States, new curricula have been developed, better teacher-training programs have been implemented, and some negative attitudes have been reversed, not only for black students but for all students who speak nonstandard varieties of English.[7] Given the record associated with the study of "proper" or standard English usage, these accomplishments are no small feats. But not enough work has yet been done on Gullah.

## Present-Day Gullah

Since the early 1920s Gullah has been known to vary region-ally; recent studies by Irma Cunningham, Patricia Nichols, Charles Joyner, Salikoko Mufwene, Ian Hancock, and me, conducted in differ-ent areas of the Sea Islands and the adjacent coast indicate that there are still distinct varieties.[8] Minor details such as consistent use of the pronoun *e*, which is applied to both sexes, and a distinctive fricative "fizzing" sound on words beginning with *w* would go unnoticed by casual observers. However, they permit the islanders to detect when one is from a different island, when one is a total outsider, and when one is trying to talk "proper," in the negative sense of the word. In fact, during my first few years on the islands, I learned that I should not try to pass myself off as an islander by an attempt to imitate the Sea Island language. While I may have had the syntax right, I was never able to perfect the accent, and it is the stress and intonation that give one away. When I asked the islanders how they were able to detect such small differences, I was often told, "I ain't know how I de know, but I de know." And they did know.

The outside pressures now exerted on the Gullah-speaking com-munities in the coastal areas of Georgia and South Carolina have cre-ated the general conditions that David DeCamp describes for post-creole speech communities (i.e., communities in which a creole is in the process of merging with a standard language). There is a corre-spondence between the dominant official language and the creole, and new educational programs and other infusions from the outside have broken down the formerly rigid social structure enough to cause social mobility and to motivate large numbers of Gullah speakers to modify their speech in the direction of standard English.[9] Given this so-ciolinguistic situation, the Sea Islands offer an ideal opportunity to investigate linguistic convergence and change.

Before proceeding further, it is important to clarify several facts about Gullah in order to distinguish it from the speech of other black Americans. First, whereas Gullah is a creole, inland black speech is defined as a dialect of English, that is, as a variant of the English language peculiar to a particular region or social context. A dialect of any given language is similar to that language in phonology, vocabu-lary, and syntax; such differences as may exist often result from regional or social variations, and most dialectal variations present few major comprehension barriers to speakers of the standard language. On the other hand, while a creole language also results from social and regional variations, a creole is similar to the primary language mainly in vocabulary; it differs in features of syntax and phonology to the extent that the creole and the primary language may be mutually unintelligible.

Secondly, despite the common West African ancestry of speakers of black English dialect, Gullah, and other creoles, isolation has tended to protect the Africanisms in the islanders' speech. As noted in Chapter 1, blacks are still in a majority on most of the Sea Islands and still enjoy the effects of both isolation and majority status. The impact of outside forces is not yet intense enough in most places to modify greatly the traditional, socially cohesive customs. And Gullah still thrives as the language of familiarity in the Sea Island communities. Even the few white families that have long made their homes on the islands speak Gullah, and readily admit to speaking it. Most native-born white is-landers say they learned Gullah as a first language from their parents, neighbors, and island playmates.

The third and perhaps most important distinction between Gullah and black dialect is in vocabulary. True, the lexicon of Gullah, like that of black dialect, is composed primarily of English words. Even so, there are a host of African-derived words in Gullah, some of which are generally unknown to inland black speakers, for example:

*gula,* "pig": Kongo  
*goober,* "peanut": Kimbundu  
*gumbo,* "okra": Tshiluba  
*gumbi,* "medicinal weed":  
    Bambara  
*heh,* "yes": Vai  
*hoodoo,* "bad luck": Hausa  
*yambi,* "yam": Vai  
*chigger,* "small flea": Wolof  
*juk, juky,* "disorderly": Wolof  
*cush,* "bread," "cake": Hausa  
*nana,* "elderly woman,"  
    "grandmother": Twi  

*nansi,* "spider": Twi  
*tote,* "to carry": Kikongo  
*chicabod,* "seesaw": Mandingo  
*unu,* "you": Igbo  
*yent,* "to lie": Umbundu  
*pinto, bento,* "coffin": Temne  
*biddy,* "small chicken": Kongo  
*buckra,* "white man": Ibebio  
*de,* "to be": Igbo  
*eh,* "yes": Igbo  
*ashantie,* "house": Ga[10]

Most of the islanders still have two kinds of given names: one used within the Sea Island community and one used in outside transactions. Mozi, Misy, Maima, Kutsey, Kisi, Lunza, Masa, Yatta, and Chineque

It is a common African practice to give people names that represent personal characteristics. It is not unusual for a Sea Islander to be named for the day of the week or month of the year in which he was born.

are among those names whose roots are traceable to West African languages. Some older island residents are named after the day of the week or month of the year when they were born. While it is very European to ask, with Shakespeare, "What's in a name?" it is very African to answer, "Everything is in a name." For example, the name Ada given to a girl child in Igbo means that the girl is the firstborn daughter. It is customary for Igbo children to be named after days of the week or given names that express sentiment: a woman who has long been unable to conceive might name a child finally born to her Ngozi, for instance, meaning "blessing" in Igbo. Some linguists have challenged Turner's work, claiming that most of the four thousand Africanisms that he listed were nicknames, or what the islanders call "basket" names.[11] Yet as DeCamp so aptly states, "Names are also a part of language and are no less capable of preserving an African heritage than are common nouns."[12]

Many of the "old words"—Africanisms—known to the older island residents are, with the "new talk," fading from use. A number of idioms are still very much apparent in daily communication, however. Consider the following list:

dark the light: the sun was set
out the light: turn the light out
hot the water: bring the water to a boil
ugly too much: very ugly
the old man bury: the old man is dead
this side: this island
do the fect to you: cause harm to come to you
can't bring the word right now: I can't remember at the moment,
    or I will not speak of it at this time
pull off my hat: I had to run
de fix for you: lie in wait for you
watchitsir!: watch your step!
day clean: daybreak
clean skin: a person with light skin color
one day mong all!: finally!
nothing for dead: nothing dying
the sun de red for down: sunset
knock em: hit
sweetmouth: flatter

rest you mouth!: shut up!
long eye: envy

Most linguists agree that lexicon is perhaps one of the most arbitrary features that languages borrow from one another, and it is in this area that they tend to borrow most extensively. As Talmy Givón has explained, when different linguistic groups come in contact, it is natural that the area of most acute linguistic conflict will be the lexicon; by borrowing words from each other, speakers resolve the communication conflict. But languages seldom borrow grammar.[13] Thus, in areas where Gullah is spoken, it is well to understand that while the lexicon is primarily English, much of the underlying grammar is rooted in West African languages.

In detailed analysis of Gullah I have used Walt Wolfram's "matrix of cruciality," selecting for discussion those features still persistent in Gullah speech.[14] Every effort has been made to present very technical material as nontechnically as possible, in order to assist readers in understanding peculiarities of Gullah speech, not only to help them appreciate the language but to suggest something of the rhythm and flow of the narratives and tales, a quality which, as I have noted, cannot be captured on paper.

## Features of Grammar

Many characteristic features of grammar and syntax set Gullah apart from other varieties of African-American speech.[15] Unlike standard English, which relies heavily on subordination to convey relationships between ideas, contemporary Gullah relies on coordination, or the combination of sentences that are short, abrupt, and loosely strung together. Gullah thus dispenses with many of the prepositions, conjunctions, adjectives, adverbs, and participles that tie together complex standard English sentences. In addition, the relationships between sentences are not necessarily specified through grammatical operations but may be left to be inferred from the usage or context.

The verb and pronoun systems are particularly distinctive in Gullah. Some distinguishing features of the verb structure include the uninflected verb, verb serialization, the introductory verb *say* [se], the complementizer *for* [fə], and verb reduplication.

## The Uninflected Verb

Gullah speakers have maintained an aspectual system with few formal markings to indicate tense. Accordingly, a single verb stem may be used to refer to a past, present, or future action. In fact, little importance is attached to the actual time when an action took place; rather, it is the mood and aspect of the action which impressed the speaker at the moment that are important. This is a pattern also common in the West African languages that contributed to Gullah—Ewe, Mandinka, Igbo, Yoruba, and others.[16]

Instead of using a system of postverbal marking, with *-ed, -s,* and *-ing,* for example, Gullah speakers use preverbal marking: the particles *de* [də], *ben* [bɛn], *bina* [bɛnə] and *don* [dɔŋ], the principal tense and aspect indicators, appear before the main verb to signal when an event occurred. Observe their appearances in the following constructions, which were obtained by asking Gullah speakers to produce semantic equivalents of English sentences that referred to shelling peas:

| English: | Gullah: |
|---|---|
| I shell them. | I shell em (tenseless). |
| She shells them. | She (e, he) de shell em. |
| I am shelling them. | I de shell em. |
| I shelled them. | I ben shell em. |
| I have been shelling them. | I bina shell em. |
| I have shelled them. | I don shell em. |
| I shelled them some time ago. | I ben don shell em. |

The preverb *de,* in *I de shell em,* can often be heard and understood as *I shelled them,* as well as *I will shell them. De* appears most frequently in contemporary Gullah speech as a replacement for present-tense forms of English *be* verbs: *am, is, are.*

## Verb Serialization

A construction common to most creole languages and still very much inherent in contemporary varieties of Gullah is verb serialization. This process involves systematically joining one, two, or even three verbs to express an idea where standard English would use one main verb and one or more additional clauses or phrases, as in the following sentences:

Gullah: I hear tell say he know some old-time story.

English: I heard it said that he knows some old-time stories. Verbs are used in Gullah to perform functions discharged by other parts of speech in standard English. While all three (*hear, say,* and *tell*) are communicative verbs, *hear* is the only main verb; *tell* performs as a participle and *say* as a connective introducing an objective clause. In this practice Gullah follows the pattern of African serializing languages of the Kwa group, such as Yoruba, Igbo, Ibebio, and Ewe. It is not uncommon in these languages to find strings of verbs, one after the other, all having the same tense or mood and all having a common subject.[17] Observe the following construction from Igbo:

Igbo: Obi kpọrọ nkụ mmadụ.
Literal translation: Obi drying wooding his person.
English: Obi is getting as hard as wood.

## The Verb *Say* [se]

Whenever possible, the Sea Island speakers tend to interrupt a narrative with reports of direct address, as opposed to the indirect reporting of information often found in standard English discourse. The word *say* is most commonly used in Gullah to introduce a direct quotation and is repeated before each clause, group of words, or single utterance, in order to assure that the listeners will recognize what follows as the exact words of another speaker. The use of *say* may be observed in Gullah as follows:

Gullah:   He tell em, say, "E ain't no deer round here."
          Say, "Where you de hunt?"

English:  He told him, "There aren't any deer around here."
He asked, "Where are you hunting?"

It is noteworthy that the word *say* has parallels in West African languages in its use as an introductory verb. In Twi, for example, *say* has not only the same function but a similar phonetic shape: [sɛ].[18]

## The Complementizer *For* [fə]

The complementizer *for* [fə] is used in Gullah to signal the infinitive. It corresponds to the English word *for* in form, but it has more variable functions. It is amenable to English translation by the modals *must* or *should* and is most commonly used to introduce clauses of purpose or intent. It appears in contexts like the following:

Gullah:  He must be born with something for see em.
For see, she could see em plain.
English: *She* must have been born with something to enable her to see them. You (must) understand, she could see them plainly. (For the pronoun switch see "The Pronominal System" below.)

It is true that some varieties of English have used *for* in similar contexts. *For* used before infinitives or even in conjunction with *to,* as in *for to,* was prevalent in English especially between 1200 and 1500, and it is apparently recorded in rural areas of England today. While *for to* has been recorded in Gullah speech, the simultaneous occurrence seem to be the exception rather than the rule, even in early descriptions of Gullah.[19] The assumption that Gullah has retained archaic features attributable to diverse areas of the British Isles is surprising, given that the Scottish, Irish, and East Anglian immigrants to America did not transmit these features to their own descendants.[20] The assumption that *for* is primarily of English origin loses more validity in light of the evidence that varieties of pidgin and creole language in West Africa today utilize the complementizer *for* in constructions similar to those in which it is used in Gullah, and there is no possibility of obsolete English influence there. Variants of *for* are common in West African languages; for example, Twi and Ewe use *fe* and Yoruba *fa,* all with syntactical functions similar to those of English *for.* This controversy (as well as some others involving Gullah and other creole languages) has theoretical import for the study of etiology in pidgin and creole languages. The form may be English or may be African, but most probably it resulted from both, since the occurrence of a similar word with similar functions is characteristic of both parent language groups.

## Verb Reduplication

Reduplication is very common in Gullah. It is used to intensify; to indicate degree, magnitude, quality, or duration; and to express great excitement. Variation in repetition is often the key to the rhythm of Sea Island speech. Words or phrases are not repeated monotonously. Rather, each word or phrase starts with a low tone, rises to a mid tone with the first repetition, and reaches a very high pitch with the second repetition. The addition of repetitions usually modifies the meaning, as in the following:

| Gullah: | small small | English: | very small |
|---|---|---|---|
| | small small small | | extremely small |
| | clean clean | | very clean |
| | wrap up wrap up | | wrap up very tightly |
| | hungry hungry | | very hungry |

Some words may be preceded or followed by *too much,* to emphasize the meaning or alter it slightly: *small too much,* for example, means "very small" or "too small." Depending on intonation, *too much* can have a positive or negative connotation; for instance, *clean too much* signifies either "very clean" or "obsessed with cleanliness."

Reduplication forms are similarly widespread and are used to express a variety of meanings in African languages belonging to the Kwa group. Creole languages in general tend to follow the structure of the substrate language (in this case African), and it seems logical to conclude that the persistence of reduplication in Gullah is indeed an African carry-over.

## The Pronominal System

In the Gullah pronominal system one can still observe clear demarcations between European and West African language practices. Whereas English employs separate pronouns to specify masculine, feminine, and neuter genders, some speakers of contemporary Gullah adhere to a system in which gender is unspecified and the same pronoun, *e* [i], may be used to refer to males and females in the nominative and genitive cases. "E blink e eye," for example, can be translated either "He blinked his eye" or "She blinked her eye." The West African languages from which Gullah is in part derived also omit case and gender distinctions between pronouns. Note the system in Igbo, for example:

Nominative: *ya₃*, "he," "she," "it"
Genitive: *ya₃* "his," "hers," "its"
Objective: *ya₃* "him," "her," "it"

This schema is somewhat simplified because it does not indicate that the Igbo pronouns *o* and *ọ* are the inseparable forms and the forms used most frequently in indirect or reported speech, whereas *ya₃* is used most often with tags, direct reports, or commands. Other variants, governed by vowel harmony or other linguistic structures, are employed as well. In Igbo and other tone languages, meaning is portrayed at least as much by the tone or manner in which something is said as by the word itself. The rhythm is inherent in the language, and in the words of an Igbo informant, "the language is actually sung." But the important fact for this discussion is that one pronoun, regardless of form, can be used whatever the case and gender. Specifications are indicated largely through context and prefixing.

The features outlined here are but a few of those distinguishing Gullah from English and known to have West African parallels. In addition to tense markers, for example, indicators of voice and number are often missing from the verb system in Gullah. Pronouns that would be expected in English may also be infrequent or absent in Gullah—for instance, the feminine pronoun *her*, the subject and object pronoun *it*, the first-person plural pronoun *us*, and the whole category of possessive pronouns. But even without further elaboration, it should be clear that an understanding of how the Sea Island language works will help in appreciating the tales and prayers that have been presented in this book, the authentic "old-time talk."

# Conclusion

[di lɔd ɛ̃ bınə muß mi mɔŋtın
bət i bın gıß mi siç.ɹɛt ɸə klɒɪəm]

*God didn't move my mountain,*
*but he gave me strength to climb it.*

During my search for Africanisms in the Sea Island culture over the past ten years, I have seen that some of the old traditions are dying out while others remain intact. Each year I see something different, hear more old tales, and learn another old word. It is hard to measure the precise impact of new pressures on the islands. But the islanders are beginning to lose their geographical isolation, and they are thus being forced to alter a culture which has existed and served them well since the first importation of African slaves to the island shores.

Some elements are resistant to change. The extended family is remaining intact because the islanders are still in a majority. Though their communities are being diluted by outsiders, their family norms are less open to invasion. The islands are still sectioned off into family communities where all persons remotely related to the family have the right to live. This housing tradition will be difficult to disrupt, though it may be easier to displace. The pressure of nearby resort areas has encouraged land take-overs at some spots, and taxation and other legal means have been used to force homeowners to leave (see Appendix 4). However, when the islanders are obliged to move, most often they relocate at a place where relatives offer them a piece of land on which to build. Thus the cohesiveness of the family structure continues to prevail.

There is continuity, too, in the religious services. Worship is shared with others who appreciate the place of religious exercises in the traditional structure of beliefs and values. The services continue to be alive, energetic, and thoroughly enjoyable. Sermons and prayers are still passed on orally from one generation to the next, rather than written down. The sermons are delivered by ministers who are natives of the island area, who speak the language, and who value the old traditions.

Basketry and marketing remain important, for two reasons. They have economic significance, but pride has also become a factor. The children learning the basket traditions now are being told that the patterns they are weaving repeat not only the patterns woven by their grandparents but those of their African ancestors before them.

Fishing and netting continue to provide livelihoods for many, though they are endangered by development and pollution of the waters. The islanders are "river and ocean" people. They gauge their workdays by the sun and by the ebb and flow of the tides. Some continue to use the marsh mud to fertilize their gardens. Others go to the banks of the ocean recesses to sit, fish, and tell tales of Ber Rabbit, tales often so vivid that many of the children swear they have actually seen him bounding down the island paths. The fishing techniques and the love and respect for the ocean are being passed on to the children along with the tales, myths, lies, and legends of island life.

The folklore and literature of the Sea Islands, unsurprisingly, are more alive on the remote islands than on the more commercialized ones. Though television, with its cartoon characters and talking pictures, is an arch rival for even the most gifted teller, on stormy days and dark, gloomy nights no one is permitted to watch television because the islanders believe that it draws electricity and increases the possibility that their homes could be struck by lightning. During these times the children are gathered and told tales of Ber Rabbit, hants, ghosts, witches, and hags, and no television program can hold an audience as spellbound as some of the island storytellers.

Gullah, the island language, is being affected by population changes, television, and the schools. Children are seldom named after days of the week any more, but most are still given two names: one to use at school and one to use at home. Many of the words familiar to the older generations are not being passed on to the children because the islanders, like most parents, want their children to attain good educations, and a good education does not include the old vocabulary. The children do, however, still learn to speak and understand Gullah: they return home from school and community to extended families where older members are responsible for their discipline and training; the church services are rendered in an elite variety of Gullah; the schoolteachers are from the islands and often chastise the children in Gullah; and most of all, the islanders are in a majority and Gullah, not standard English or a variety thereof, is the accepted language of the community. In the near future, therefore, some version of Gullah will probably continue to exist as the language of the home and of the community.

Finally, the islanders remain as conservative about their culture as they ever were. As I have noted, they are hostile to strangers, and word of outsiders carries quickly. No one, black, white, or otherwise, can escape their cultural interrogations. They will want to know who each newcomer is, and why this person has arrived. But it is not true, I learned, that the islanders will remain hostile. Once one establishes oneself within a community (which often takes years to do), one will receive all possible warmth and hospitality and all the help one might need to carry out one's work.

In writing this book I promised to tell the story of the islanders as I saw it, and to the best of my ability, that is what I have done.

The end of that one!

# Appendix 1

---

# An Interview: Catching Fish

The ancient fishing methods explained in this interview are reminiscent of those found in Nigeria and other African countries near large bodies of water. I actually observed the drumming and spearing technique among the Igbo and Ibebio of northern Nigeria. Juanita Jackson, Sabra Slaughter, and J. Herman Blake also write of this continuing fishing practice on the Sea Islands.[1]

The informant was a retired tradesman and a very important member in the church community. He said that he learned these practices from his father, and his father had learned them from the "old people" before him.

The interview has been edited slightly for clarity.

Mr. Daniel Dent
Wadmalaw Island, South Carolina
1983

INFORMANT: To catch mullet fish, we goes in the river. Everything still. The water still. Make a few throw with the cast net, and you haven't catch anything. So you get up on the side of boat and you beat on side with you oars, or paddle. And you just keep beating—[you] call em dolphin, we call em horsemen—then beat until the porpoise come around. After the porpoise come around, then the mullet fish will come to the shallow water. [Then] you cast for catch em. You don't catch much fish without the horseman. The porpoise have to be around. The only way to get the porpoise, man—[you] don't see them—you beat some, on the side of the boat, and they'll hear you miles for miles under the water.

Fishermen often travel among the islands in rowboats. These two men are preparing to row from Yonges Island to Wadmalaw.

INTERVIEWER: How does the sound go?

INFORMANT: (Tapping out a steady beat on his chair) You can't hear the sound.

LISTENER: You can't get the right sound. Under water de different sound.

INFORMANT: (Taps again) Something like that. (Taps again) Here's the beat. This the way it sound. But a little bit lighter because e not on the water. You on the boat with a paddle. So that the way you get your fish when you fishes in deep water. You call the dolphin to the shore by paddle beating on the boat. So many time I done that for a living—until I can't number em.

INTERVIEWER: You called the dolphin three things?

INFORMANT: I call em a horseman or a porpoise. The way I learn, I learn from the old people.

INTERVIEWER: You call him a horseman?

INFORMANT: Uh hum. In fact, e *is* a horseman for a workman. See? You understand what I'm talk about now?

INTERVIEWER: A horseman?

INFORMANT: A horseman, yeah. Someting that most people call [a thing with] four feet. But the man [part] is a man. All right?

INTERVIEWER: Do you know any other fishing methods?

INFORMANT: I knows gig [gill] net [smoke fishing]. The way I use to, when I come up [was growing up], I was too poor to buy a lantern. So we just [went] out [in the] winter time, and those who had tires on they car, [if the tires were] no good, we use that for a light. And we goes in river. Sometimes the wind blows, e blind you with the smoke. But we had manage to catch many bushel of trouts and many bushel of fish with four-prong or three-prong gig. Caught many bushel fish that way. Just use a little tar for light by night, and we gelds [stick] fish in the water.

LISTENER: Catch em by stick em with that fork.

INTERVIEWER: Do you know any other ways?

INFORMANT: Yeah, I had did this back in Hoover time when tings was bad. We didn't had, couldn't get a cast hook the way I want em. I had takes someting we call hog wire and put em cross the river. When the tide comes up, you goes and cut muckle mish [bush] and drop em behind the wire to hold the fish on that side when e [the tide] goes down because we didn't had a gill net to put over

Sea Island children are intimately familiar with the ocean and learn the art of casting and netting as early as the age of three.

river. Time was for tight, we couldn't buy a gill net. So what I be do, take hog wire and put em across em when tide low. When the tide get high, we take the bush and put em in the front of the wire. When the water start for go back, the fish can't get through, de stop on that side.

# Appendix 2

---

# Buh Rabbit en' de Lawd

What follows is the tale "Ber Rabbit and the Lord" from Chapter 3, reconstructed in the Gullah of a century ago. A comparison of the two versions will show how the language has changed in the interim.

I am grateful to Mrs. Virginia Mixon Geraty, who suggested and prepared the transcription, for her time, willingness, and patience.

One time Buh Rabbit gone tuh de Lawd fuh git mo' ecknowledge, mo' wisdum. En' de Lawd tell Buh Rabbit, "Awright! Uh wan' you fuh fetch me ennyt'ing wuh w'ite. Ennyt'ing w'ite."

Rabbit gone een de fiel', en' 'e gone en' meet Buh Paa'tridge dey dey, 'e hab uh bag, en' 'e tell Buh Paa'tridge: "Uh betchuh all ub you, all ub you ent able fuh full'up dishyuh bag."

Paa'tridge say, "How you mean?"

Run een de bag en' see kin you full'um up."

De paa'tridge 'pread 'e wing, run een de bag en' full'um up. Buh Rabbit pit'um 'cross 'e shoulduh en' cya'um tuh de Lawd. "Awright!" 'E gone sen'um back. Buh Rabbit sen' Buh Paa'tridge back.

"Well, now, Buh Rabbit, Uh wan' you fuh fetch me—Uh wan' you fuh fetch me—uh rattlesnake!" Dainjus!!! 'E pit Buh Rabbit weh 'e dainjus, fuh true!

Buh Rabbit tell'um, "Awright!"

Buh Rabbit gone een de fiel' en' fin' uh rattlesnake, en' 'e hab uh cane en' 'e tell Buh Rattlesnake: "Buh Snake, oonuh ent—oonuh ent long ez dis cane." Buh Rattlesnake run 'long 'side de cane.

Buh Rabbit say, "No! Uh yent mean fuh do'um so. Uh wan' oonuh fuh run een'um."

Buh Snake run een de cane—tshht, Buh Rabbit stop up de hole en' cya'um tuh de Lawd.

'E say, "Awright, now, Buh Rabbit, you pit een fibe. You good! You good 'nuf! Now Uh wan' you, Buh Rabbit, Uh wan' you fuh fetch me uh 'gatuh tail tuh me—f'um de watuh."

Rabbit say, "Uh kin fetch dat!"

Rabbit drunk-up 'ese'f en' 'e gone down tuh de ribbuh, en' 'e tell Buh 'Gatuh, say, "Buh 'Gatuh???"

Buh 'Gatuh say, "Buh Rabbit, weh oonuh gwine?"

'E say, "Uh gwine obuh Adale—en' uh yent hab no way fuh git dey dey. Uh yent gots no boat."

Buh 'Gatuh tell Buh Rabbit, say, "Jump 'puntop me head. Uh gwi' cya' oonuh obuh dey."

Buh Rabbit jump 'puntop Buh 'Gatuh head. W'en Buh 'Gatuh git 'cross todduh sho', Buh Rabbit knock Buh 'Gatuh een 'e head en' knock out all 'e teet', en' cya'um tuh de Lawd.

Buh Lawd say, "Awright!"

Buh Rabbit say, "Wuh you wan' me fuh do 'gen?"

Say, "Uh wan' you mus' fetch me some cow milk."

Rabbit say, "Awright!"

Rabbit bex de cow en' de cow run 'roun', run 'roun', run 'roun', en twu'l 'roun', 'roun', 'roun' 'e foot. Rabbit graff'um! De cow fall down! De rabbit git 'tween 'e laig en' milk'um, en' 'e cya' de milk tuh Buh Lawd.

"Awright!" Buh Rabbit say, "Now Lawd!"

"Uh wan' you mus' fetch me some bull milk."

"Awright!"

Buh Rabbit jump down dey dey en' bex de bull, 'e bex de bull—bex de bull. Say, "Bull, oonuh cyan' do same lukkuh de cow." Say, "Uh wan' oonuh fuh run 'roun' dis tree."

De bull run 'roun' de tree en' de bull fall down. De rabbit try fuh milk de bull. 'E gone back tuh de Lawd—'e call, "Lawd, Uh gots de milk."

De Lawd say, "Buh Rabbit, weh de hell you see bull gib milk?"

Buh Rabbit, de same milk wuh 'e cya', de cow milk, de Lawd tek dat milk en' 'E fling'um behime Buh Rabbit tail, en' cause'um fuh w'ite. En' 'E tell Buh Rabbit, "Go 'head, [rabbit] en' dog condishun sameso. Ef de bush crack you haffuh gone!!!"

# Appendix 3

---

# Phonetic Text:
# The Soul and the Spirit

The following text is included in this study primarily to show the language in context. It manifests many phonological, syntactical, and morphological constructions characteristic of creole languages.[1] The English version following the transcription obscures many of the creole patterns; consequently, a word-for-word translation accompanies each line of phonetic script to illustrate underlying creole constituents such as the complementizer [fə], the introductory verb [sie], the future marker [go], and many other constructions.

This passage reveals specific segmental phonological phenomena, for example, vowel epenthesis, consonant reduction, assimilation, and various phones corresponding to, or substituted for, such English phones as /β/ for /w/; /ɸ/ for /f/; /t/ for initial /ð/ and /θ/; and /ç/ and /ʃ/ for /s/. No effort has been made to eliminate false starts, deviant words, or stuttering. It is extremely difficult to hear certain sequences because of interference of birds and other outdoor noises on the tape. In such cases ellipsis dots indicate that a short passage, usually no more than a few words, has been deleted because of unintelligibility.

Terminal junctures and pauses have been indicated by a slash (/). Creaky voice is indicated by a wavy underline ( ∿∿∿ ).

Hyphens join two or more words run together in the transcription.

English translations of the preverbal markers and the third-person pronominal forms often misrepresent the creole utterance. The following notations are accordingly used to symbolize these forms:

(3 ♂ n) third-person masculine nominative
(3 ♀ n) third-person feminine nominative

(3 Ø n)   third-person neuter nominative
(3 ♂ o)   third-person masculine objective
(3 ♀ o)   third-person feminine objective
(3 Ø o)   third-person neuter objective
(PrC)      present continuative   /də/
(PaC)      past                          /bɪnə/
(T)          tense indicator          /bɪn/
(L)          locative                    /də/

### di soəl ɛn di speɪt

1. lɪsn mi gʊd nɔu / βɛn ju daɪ nɪs wɔ̃l / jusi / dɪ dɪ dɪ so·əl
   *Listen me good now: when you die in-this world, you see,*
   *the, the, the soul*
2. əβə män go ɦiom dʊ di kɪŋdəm ə gɔd / bɔt jʊə speit
   *of-a man go home to the Kingdom of God, but your spirit*
3. stɪls iə ɔn ɔʔt / ɛn ɪɸ ju βədɪ dɛβəl ɪn ɒl jʊə diez /
   *still's here on earth. And if you was-the devil in all your*
   *days,*
4. jʊə speit /ätə jʊ died / joə speit kə du di siem tɪŋ / jʊə speit
   *your spirit, after you dead, your spirit can do the same thing,*
   *your spirit.*
5. jʊə soəl ɔ̈p dɛ / bɔt jʊə speit dɛ ɹɛʔ dɔŋ də iə βɪd
   *Your soul up there, but your spirit (L) right down (L) here*
   *with*
6. di bɒɾi / ɛn däs də wɔn gɔ gɔ du də ɸɛk tu jʊ / jʊ si nɔ nɔ
   *the body. And that's the one gone, gone do the effect to you.*
   *You see now now*
7. das das βɒɪ ɒɪ sie dɪs nɔ / ə lɒs ä pipŭ
   *that's that's why I say this now. A lot of people*
8. dõn biliɸ / sie sie sieiz no guos / iz guos dɛə /bɔt nɔ sensz
   *don't believe. Say say say-is no ghost. Is ghost there. But*
   *now since*
9. di ʔɑɾəmobɪl n tɪŋ kɔm / n gɪt dɪ hɒɪβie nɔ / jʊsidiz diz tɪŋ
   *the automobile and thing come and get the highway now,*
   *you-see-these, these thing*
10. käɪnə tɛk tu wʊd / äɪ mɛmbə wɔnäɪt / βi βi bɪn ɔut
    *kind-of take to wood. I member one-night we, we (T) out*

11. n di ɹəβə / wɔʰɒnˀ wɔ wɔtʃɛkɪn ʃiβɪms / ɛnəβɛn ɒɪ lʊk / wɔ ɵ̃
    *in the river, was-hunt, was, was-catching shrimps. And-ah-*
    *when I look, was a*

12. mɪn mi ɸɔ̈s kɔ̈zn ɹɛɾɔpdil / βi bɪn ɪn kɹɪk / ɛn βɛn ɒɪ lʊk bɛk
    *me-and me first cousin, right-up-the-hill, we (T) in crick. And*
    *when I look back*

13. bəˀɒɪn βi / i wɔ̈z ə kɔɸɔm bɪn bəhɒɪn βi / dɛ nätʃəl
    *behind we, (3 ø n) was a coffin (T) behind we. The natural-*

14. bɔn kɔɸɔm gɛl ʃɑin dɔŋ dɪ kɹik /
    *born coffin, gal, shine down the crick.*

15. ɛn βɛn βɛn i gɛt ɔpə kloə tʊ βi ɸã ju tʊ da kä jõna / i tek'
    *And when, whn, (3 ð n) get up-a close to we far you to the*
    *car-yonder, (3 ð n) take*

16. daˀma·ʃ / ɛn daˀ maʃ bɪnə lie dɔŋ dis / lie dɔŋ dʒɪs lɛk dät /
    *that-marsh. And that marsh (PaC) lay down just, lay down*
    *just like that.*

17. ɛn ɒɪ bɪnə sɪɾɔŋ ɛn ɒɪ ẽ nõ ɒɪ bɪnə ɪnəsi / si . . . /
    *And I (PaC) sit-down and I ain't know I (PaC) in-a-seat.*
    *See . . .*

18. jie / də nɛ·tʃal kɔɸɪn / də nɛ·tʃəl kɔɸɪn kɔmɪn dɔŋdiɹɪβə /
    siβɪm
    *yeah, the natural coffin, the natural coffin coming down-the-*
    *river, swim.*

19. dasəspeɪt nɔu / jie / kɔmɪn dɔŋ də ɹɪβə / ɛn βɛn / ˀɒˀə βi /
    dɪsbɔi
    *That's-a-spirit now. Yeah. Coming down the river. And*
    *when—after we, this-boy*

20. tɔk βirəm / hidis / çɪɸ wɔn sɐid oβəndə mäʃ jusi / ɛn hi sitɛt
    *talk with-(3 ø o), (3 ø n)-just shave one side over-in-the*
    *marsh, you-see. And (3 ø n) start*

21. tʊ lie da maʃ dɔŋ / ɛn lɛɸ da maʃɛn gönɔpnɪiedʒ ədawʊd /
    *to lay that marsh down, and left that marsh-and gone-up-in-*
    *the-edge of-that-wood,*

22. ɛn laˀ da wʊd bɪn bɐut ɸɔ ɸɔm βi·z də kɹɪk /
    *and Lord, that wood (T) about far from we-as the crick.*

23. ɛn ju kədə jɛri ɔu i kieɔntɔpida ɪn da wʊd /
    *And you could-have heard how (3 ø n) carry-on-top-of-that,*
    *in that wood.*

24. βiel nɔdiztinɪzdɛ nɔ / nɔ ɛβibodi kɛ̃ çɔ̈əm /
    *Well now-these-thing-is-there now. No, everybody can't see-them.*

25. bɔt ju gɒt ɸiɫɪn ju ʔkŋ çɔ̈əm / βiel ɒɪ äd wɔn dɔrə . . . no ɒɪ
    ɦäd wɔn dɔrə /
    *But you got feeling, you can see-them. Well, I had one daughter, . . . no, I had one daughter*

26. ɪnnu jɔk ɹüit nɔu / n hi kʊrə ʒtɛnɛni iβinɪn / ɛn ʃuə ju /
    *in-New York right now, and (3 ♀ n) could stand-any evening and show you,*

27. n ʃuə ju dɪ dɪ də pɜsn / ŋgə ʃö ju tuətɹi pɜsn / çɔˀm ɹɛit çjɒndə
    *and show you the, the, the person, and-could show you two-three person./ "See-(3 ♂ o) right yonder,*

28. dɛ̈dɪ də stɛnɔp / ɛn ɒɪ kʊdn ʃɔəm ɸə çieß mɒɪ dɒɪŋ lɒɪɸ
    *Daddy, (PrC) stand-up," and I couldn't see-(3 ♂ o) for save my dying life,*

29. ɛndä gjɛl bɪn dä βie bɪn dä βie til / dɛ̈m tɪŋ justə ɸɹɒɪdem /
    *and-that gal (T) that way, (T) that way til them thing use-to frightened-(3 ♀ o),*

30. ɛn dɛn ɒɪ kiɛm tʊ dɪ / ɒɪ kiɛm
    *and then I carry-(3 ♀ o) to the, I carry-(3 ♀ o)*

31. tə de ɦɒsipɪrɪ / ɛn βɒ nɛ̈m pipl du βirəm nɛ / ɒɪ dö no /
    *to the hospital. And what them people do with-(3 ♀ o) there, I don't know.*

32. bɒ ɸɔ̈m ɔpdä tɒɪm ɪn ɔpnɔ / ʃi neßə dɪ si nɔn nɔmo / . . .
    *But from up-that time and up-now, (3 ♀ n) never did see none no-more. . . .*

33. hi mɔs bi bɔ̈n βɪd sɔmp ɸə ʃɔəm /
    *(3 ♀ n) must be born with something for see(3 ø o).*

34. ɸə si ʃi kʊrə ʃɔəm ple·en / juno / iʔ i ʃɔəm nɛ·tʃəl juno /
    *For see, (3 ♀ n) could see-(3 ø o) (it) plain, you-know, (3 ♀ n), (3 ♀ n) see-(3 ø o) (it) natural, you-know.*

35. didɪs də sitanɔpdʰɛi ʃɔ̈m / jie ɛndɛnɒm / βiel ə o əlɒtsa pʰipl ə
    *Just-just (PrC) stan-up-there-(3 ♀ n) see-(3 ø o). Yeah. And-then-ah, well, a, oh, a-lot-of people, a,*

36. əholɒ·tsa pʰipl jugoβɪdnɔ kɛ̃ ʃɔ̈m / kɛ 'ʃɔ̈mɛn tʰɛ / ju 'tʰuə /
    *a-whole-lot-of people you-go-with now can see-(3 ø o), can see-(3 ø o)-and tell you too!*

37. si si da pɜsn jɒna / jieə / jieə /das ɹëit / jiə ju kʊ
    *"See, see that person yonder." Yeah, yeah, that's right. Yeah,*
    *you could*

38. ɸɪləm / jiə . . . mũ? / das di ol dɛβəl / βiel nɔnɔ / ju no
    *feel-(3 ♂ o) Yeah . . . muh, that's the old devil. Well now-*
    *now, you know*

39. βɒɪ ɒɪ tɔk bɔ? sɵmtɐɪm ju go bəjəsɛɸ / ɪɸ ju dis wɒk /
    *why I talk but sometime you go by-yourself. If you just walk.*

40. n sɵmtɐɪm ju ɸɪl 'timəɹɪdʒ / sɵmtɒɪ jʊ ɸɪl lɐka jʊ ɦiə /
    *and sometime you feel timeridge, sometime you feel like your*
    *hair*

41. lʊklɐi / ju ɸil / ju gɪt 'timə,ɹɪdʒ . . . / das ɹɐit /
    *look-like you feel you get timeridge . . . that's right.*

42. βiel ju si ə / jʊəspeɪt hɪt da iβəl ɸɛla / ɛn jʊə speɪt kɔm bɛk
    tʊjʊ /
    *Well, you see, ah, your-spirit hit that evil fellow. And your*
    *spirit come back to-you.*

43. dʒɪs läk ə βɛn ju go ɪn bed dɪ nɐit ɸə silip
    *Just like a, when you go in bed the night to sleep,*

44. βɛnjugoɪnbedinɐit / ɸə tiek ə ɹɛs / βel də speit
    *when-you-go-in-bed-the-night for take a rest, well, the spirit*

45. lɛɸ dɪ bɒɾɪ / si βɛn jʊə speit lɛɸ dɪ bɒɾl / jʊə
    *left the body. See, when your spirit left the body your*

46. speit go ɪn dɪɸɵn pät ə dɪs kɔntɹi / ɔloβə / ɛn dɛn sɔmtäɪm
    *spirit go in different part of this country. All-over. And then*
    *sometime*

47. βen də fɪɪt dä iβəl speit / βen ju çiəm ɹɔn / kɔm bɛk də ju
    *when (PrC) hit that evil spirit, when you see-(3 ø o) run,*
    *come back to you*

48. ɛn mɛk̩ ju skie njʊə bed / sɔmtɒɪm ju mä? ɦɒlə sɐirəsɵmlɛkdɛt
    *and make you scare in-your bed. Sometime you may holler*
    *beside-some-like-that.*

49. si jʊə speit kɔm bɛk nju ɸɹäin /
    *See, your spirit come back an-you frighten.*

50. no ju kɛ̃ silip si / ɛn dɛn ju k̩ɛ̃ βiekɵ̃p / dispeit dɵ̃
    *No, you can't sleep, see, and then you can't wake-up. The-*
    *spirit don't*

51. kɵ̃m bɛk tʊ jʊ / nɔ ɪɸ də speit dɵ̃ kɔm bɛk tʊ jʊ / jʊ nuo ju

*come back to you. Now if the spirit don't come back to you,
you know you*

52. dɛ / ɪn ɔrə wʊd / ju ẽ die oβə fiɪə / nɔdä tɹ̥uɸ / nɔ /
    *there. In other word, you ain't there over here. Now-that
    truth, now.*

53. nɔ däs tɹ̥uɸ / ju gɪt dɪ bɒɪbl ɛn ju ɹirəm / däs tɹ̥uɸ /
    *Now that's truth. You get the Bible and you read-(3 ɸ o).
    That's truth.*


Listen well now: when you die, you see, the soul of a man goes
home to the Kingdom of God, but your spirit remains here on earth.
And if you were an evildoer all of your life, then after you die, your
spirit can continue doing the same kind of evil. Your soul is in heaven,
but your spirit remains here on earth with the body, and that's the one
that will harm you.

You see, I speak of this now because a great many people don't
believe. They say that ghosts do not exist. But they do exist. But now,
since the automobile and other transportation has overrun the highways, these spirits have sought refuge in the woods.

I remember one night we, my first cousin who lives up on the hill
and I, were out in the river catching shrimps. And when we looked
behind us, we saw a coffin, a natural coffin, Miss, shining down the
crick. And when it came as close to us as the distance between you and
that car, it disappeared into the marsh. The marsh separated from the
burden and lay open. And I found myself sitting down without
knowing when I became seated. . . . Yes, it was a natural coffin swim-
ming down the river. Now that was a spirit coming down the river.
Well, after [my cousin] spoke with it, it turned sharply to one side,
flattened the marsh, and went up in the wood's edge only a distance as
far as from us to the crick, and Lord, you could hear the confusion as it
carried on in those woods.

Well, these things do exist. No, everybody can't see them. But if
you are sensitive you can feel them. I have a daughter in New York
today, and she could on any evening show you one ghost or two or
three ghosts. "See it standing right there, Daddy!" But I couldn't see it
to save my dying life. But she had always been frightened by ghosts.
Finally, I took her to the hospital, and I don't know what the hospital

personnel did to her, but since that time she never has seen any more. . . . She must have been born with something to be able to see them because she could stand and see them plainly and naturally. Yes, well, a great many people, a great many people that one associates with now can see them. They can see them and point them out to you. "See that person over there." Yes, yes. . . . That's the old devil. Well now, you know that I often exaggerate, but sometimes you walk alone, and if you feel a tremor as if your hair feels strangely on edge . . . that's right. Well, you see, your spirit has touched that evil spirit and your spirit has come back to your body.

For example, when you go to bed at night to sleep, to rest, the spirit leaves the body and when it leaves it goes in different parts of this country, all over the world. Sometimes when it comes in contact with an evil spirit, it runs back and scares you. You see, your spirit comes back and frightens you and you can neither sleep nor wake up. But if the spirit doesn't return to the body, you know that you are in heaven. In other words, you are not in the body here on earth. Now that's the truth. You get your Bible and read it. That is the truth.

# Appendix 4

# The Land Question

As the islanders often put it, "Everything change up now." One of the major areas of change in recent years has been in the use and ownership of land in the islands. "Primarily," comments Ed Brown, an attorney practicing in Charleston County who grew up on Wadmalaw,

> the land is changing hands because history has created a division between those people who own the land and those people who want to buy land. And if a developer comes in here with forty thousand dollars for ten acres of land, which might appear at first blush to be a lot of money, the landowner is perhaps inclined to take the forty thousand dollars and part with title to the land. That happens. I don't know that that is a bad thing. I think that what it does do is it creates a problem for the person who has sold the land, because if you are not sophisticated in terms of handling the forty thousand dollars, then you lose it rather quickly, whereas the land would be there forever.[1]

The relationship of black people to land in general has considerable significance. Various studies and reports trace the origins of many of the current domestic ills of the United States to the surge of southern blacks into urban areas as the rural southern economy found that under existing social arrangements, it could no longer employ large numbers of small farmers, sharecroppers, tenants, and unskilled farm laborers. In the 1960s alone, more than 1.3 million blacks left the South, and during the previous decade the number was even greater.[2]

The population that remains behind on the islands is having to adjust to the incoming population of resort residents, as well as resort development for tourism. Developers have not been responsive to local needs. Seabrook was the first of the islands to be opened up as a resort.

The original owner of the island, one of the major church denominations, sold it to a group of developers, who in turn sold it to a second group, from New York. No input from the community was requested, and a great deal of hostility resulted. When developers came to Kiawah to create a much larger resort area, they expressed readiness to meet community needs and asked for a list. The time available to come up with this list was brief, but island leaders working with Bill Jenkins, a long-time activist in land issues, did manage to set out six or seven mostly minor suggestions. "We did it in good faith," notes Jenkins. "I think we were more in good faith than they were, because some of those things we are still trying to get."

"I remember as a little boy," says Ed Brown, "that you could purchase perhaps an acre of land for two hundred dollars. Today that's just unheard of. So the very basic thing that gives the islands their wealth, namely, the property, is increasing in value, but we need to develop a methodology by which that can be properly managed and the profits therefrom, if there are to be profits, channeled back into the islands for their development." He adds, "I see good things. I'm an eternal optimist. I think that the future will prove to be very fruitful . . . if we can learn from the mistakes." Yet he does not deny that there have been mistakes, for instance, the absence of "a working rapport between the people who operate these resorts and the people who in fact live on these islands, and who have lived there for quite some time."

Land is being taken out of production. Acreage once used to grow food is now restricted and controlled by high taxes and county regulations implemented in response to development. Small livestock farmers located next to tracts under new ownership may be pressured to sell out if their activities seem incompatible with the projects of the developers. Lands are lost, too, when people unused to record keeping lose tax receipts and forget to pay yearly bills, or when land descends to heirs who have moved away and have no interest in it.

Bill Jenkins has provided an illustration of what can happen when developers are more interested in a piece of property than its legal owners:

There's seventy-nine acres of land down at Johns Island airport. . . . Developers . . . did some research and found out who were some of the people who were involved in that property. [One of them] found a wino in New York City and just walked up to him and said, "I heard you own some property on Johns Island." The guy thought he was kidding because he had never been to Johns Island. So he just started laughing. [The developer] said, "I'm serious. You get a witness and come with me and I will give you five hundred dollars for what you own." So this guy, you know, he thought Santa Claus. So he got one of his friends and they went downtown, and he had everything probated, signed it off, and the people came down here and created all kinds of problems for the rest of the family. Eventually, they had to end up selling that land . . . because with this property, when the families are so large, most of the time you can't even get all of the family together, so they could agree who's going to get the swampland, who's going to get the house, who's going to get the waterfront. . . . But the court could sell all of the land and divide the money equally. And so, when this land developer bought this land . . . , he came down here and he wanted his portion. . . . He is now one of the heirs. But [he and the family] cannot agree on which piece. . . . Then he goes back to the court and says, "We can't reach an agreement." And if you can't reach an agreement, then the court will come in and put it up for sale.

Obviously, the question of land retention is directly tied to the education of the landowners about the legal responsibilities involved. For more than twenty years, groups have been operating in that interest throughout the Sea Islands and the rural South. In 1970 Professor Robert Browne, who was then studying the loss of black land in the South for the Black Economic Research Center in New York (he is now at Howard University), was able to obtain a million dollars from a private donor to organize the National Emergency Land Fund. The fund has focused on educating black landowners about their responsibilities, helping them express themselves, putting land into production, and resisting aggressive development.

The fund has worked in conjunction with the Penn Center on St. Helena Island, South Carolina, one of the oldest institutions established for the education of blacks in the United States. Penn School began by teaching newly freed slaves and continued as the only high school for black children on the island. In 1948 the bulk of its programs were transferred to the county public school system, but most of its community outreach activities were continued. The Penn Center, currently directed by Emory Campbell, acts as an information and referral source, provides such social services as visiting families to help them select food crops, and educates in matters including use of land and landownership.

Bill Jenkins was working for Penn Community Services in the early 1970s when he helped put together a program called Black Land Services, in response to a number of requests for help in retaining ownership of land. He is now active in the South Carolina Land Owners' Association, an offshoot of the National Association of Land Owners, which presently operates only in Mississippi and Alabama. Faced with serious cutbacks in funding and manpower, the South Carolina Land Owners' Association is not able to be as active as it once was, but Jenkins and co-worker Joe McDermott continue their educational activities in the islands on a reduced scale.

The desire of the dominant society to reclaim the Sea Islands, though shortsighted, nonetheless seems likely to prevail. As Ed Brown puts it, "The industry is there." The displacement that has already occurred will have long-term repercussions. "The social consequences of the pressures from development on the Sea Islands will be seen another five to ten to fifteen years," notes Emory Campbell. "It's subtle now but we at Penn Center see it as a very serious problem— serious today as it is going to be serious in another ten to fifteen years."

The islanders' ineffectiveness in resisting the often reckless advances of developers must be laid at the door of the very insularity that for so long protected their culture. Adherence to traditional ways has by and large robbed them of the ability to respond to the intrusion with equal and opposite force. The price they are paying now is one more legacy of slavery.

# Notes

## Preface

1. For a note on the usefulness of interdisciplinary approaches see David DeCamp, "Toward a Generative Analysis of a Post-Creole Speech Continuum," in *Pidginization and Creolization of Languages,* ed. Dell Hymes (Cambridge: Cambridge University Press, 1971), p. 369.

2. For a detailed discussion of field procedures in general see Kenneth Goldstein, *A Guide for Field Workers in Folklore* (Hatboro, N.C.: Folklore Assoc., 1964).

3. See ibid., p. 21.

4. Juanita Jackson, Sabra Slaughter, and J. Herman Blake, "The Sea Islands as a Cultural Resource," *Black Scholar,* March 1974, pp. 32–39.

5. For further discussion of entrance into Sea Island communities see Patricia Nichols, "Linguistic Change in Gullah: Sex, Age, and Mobility" (Ph.D. diss., Stanford University, 1976).

6. Goldstein, *Guide for Field Workers,* p. 173.

## Introduction

1. The titles *Mr.* and *Miss* have more significance in Sea Island communities than they do outside. They are used in daily interaction with those who are felt to have earned particular respect, becoming part of their names.

2. See Lorenzo D. Turner, *Africanisms in the Gullah Dialect* (Chicago: University of Chicago Press, 1949), pp. 11–12.

## Chapter 1

1. Jackson, Slaughter, and Blake, "The Sea Islands as a Cultural Resource," p. 32.

2. These estimates were derived primarily from the Berkeley-Charleston-Dorchester (BCD) Council of Governments' *Report on Economically Less Developed Areas in the Berkeley Charleston Dorchester Region,* 1980.

3. For a detailed discussion of the folk life and language of Sandy Island and the

surrounding area see Nichols, "Linguistic Change in Gullah"; and Charles Joyner, *Down by the Riverside: A South Carolina Slave Community* (Urbana: University of Illinois Press, 1984).

4. BCD Council of Governments, *Regional Housing Market Analysis,* 1979, p. 2.

5. Waccamaw Regional Planning and Development Council, *Waccamaw Regional Housing Element,* 1977, p. 8.

6. BCD, *Regional Housing Market Analysis,* p. 21.

7. The residents of Sandy Island have requested a bridge from the local government, but at this writing none is expected in the near future. At present all building materials, appliances, vehicles, and the like must be brought from the mainland by barge. And though residents enjoy the seclusion during the spring and summer, they complain—the children particularly—about being ferried across the river during the freezing rains that frequent the Carolina coast in winter.

8. For a discussion of the demographic characteristics of the Sea Island area see Elizabeth Donnan, *Documents Illustrative of the History of the Slave Trade to America,* vol. 4 (Washington, D.C.: Carnegie Institution of Washington, 1930); Turner, *Africanisms in the Gullah Dialect;* Philip D. Curtin, *The Atlantic Slave Trade* (Madison: University of Wisconsin Press, 1969); and Peter H. Wood, *Black Majority: Negroes in Colonial South Carolina from 1690 through the Stone Rebellion* (New York: Alfred A. Knopf, 1974).

9. Many hags, ghosts, and spirits are thought to haunt these highways, and some islanders fear them much more than the alligators, wolves, rattlesnakes, and other creatures which may prowl along the swamp roads at night.

10. Merrill G. Christophersen, *Biography of an Island* (Fennimore, Wis.: Westburg Assoc., 1976).

11. Sandy Island, in Georgetown County, is inhabited entirely by African-Americans. However, some Sea Islands just north of Charleston and closer to the coast, such as Pawleys, Sullivans, and the Isle of Palms, are peopled primarily by whites.

12. Marina Wikramanayake, *A World in Shadow: The Free Black in Antebellum South Carolina* (Columbia: University of South Carolina Press, 1973), pp. 158–59.

13. Jackson, Slaughter, and Blake, "The Sea Islands as a Cultural Resource," p. 33.

14. Frederic Bancroft, *Slave Trading in the Old South* (Baltimore: J. J. Furst Co., 1931), pp. 359–60. For further discussion of the slave trade in the Sea Island area see Georgia Writers Project, *Drums and Shadows* (Athens: University of Georgia Press, 1940; reprint, Westport, Conn.: Greenwood Press, 1973) p. xviii; Wood, *Black Majority;* and Joyner, *Down by the Riverside.*

15. BCD, *Regional Housing Market Analysis,* p. 19.

16. BCD, *Report on Economically Less Developed Areas,* p. 14.

17. Ibid., p. 13.

18. Ibid., p. 18.

19. June Manning Thomas, "The Impact of Corporate Tourism on Gullah Blacks: Notes on Issues of Employment," *Phylon* 41, no. 1 (Spring 1980): 4, 5.

20. BCD, *Report on Economically Less Developed Areas,* pp. 13, 17.

21. Thomas, "Impact of Corporate Tourism," p. 6.

22. Quoted in Mason Crum, *Gullah: Negro Life in the Carolina Sea Islands* (Du-

rham, N.C.: Duke University Press, 1940), pp. 321–22. The original source for this order is the *Report of the Commissioner of the Bureau of Refugees, Freedmen, and Abandoned Lands,* 39th Cong., 1st sess., 1865–66, Exec. Doc. 11, p. 10.

23. Guion Johnson, *A Social History of the Sea Islands with Special References to St. Helena Island, South Carolina* (Chapel Hill: University of North Carolina Press, 1930), p. 18.

24. Though many writers have stated that rice was a Sea Island crop (see, for example, Wood, *Black Majority;* and Jackson, Slaughter, and Blake, "The Sea Islands as a Cultural Resource"), Professor Charles Joyner has indicated to me (through personal communication) that rice was grown not on the Sea Islands but in rice fields adjoining nearby mainland rivers. Rice requires fresh water, and the flooding and draining of rice fields require freshwater rivers moved by ocean tides. Thus Sandy Island had rice fields but the ocean islands did not.

25. Wood, *Black Majority,* p. 59.

26. Ibid., p. 59.

27. Ruth Finnegan, *Limba Stories and Storytelling* (Oxford: Oxford University Press, 1969).

28. Rice is normally eaten for breakfast, lunch, and dinner in variation with different meats, gumbos, greens, and sauces, many of which are still prepared and eaten on the islands in traditional fashions. Two carry-overs, for example, are a kind of okra soup called *ofey okra* in Igbo and a turnip green dish prepared with bits of meat, onion, hot peppers, and pepper sauce that has its counterpart in Yoruba, Igbo, and Ibebio cultures. In Africa these vegetable and meat dishes are eaten with *fufu* or *gari,* a soft substance about the consistency of bread dough. On the islands, instead of fufu and gari, corn bread is served with the greens or okra soup; small bits are pinched off, mashed together with the fingers, and then dipped and rolled in the vegetable sauce.

29. Guion Johnson, *History of the Sea Islands,* p. 26.

30. Quoted in Crum, *Gullah,* p. 70.

31. This practice was also observed by Jackson, Slaughter, and Blake; see "The Sea Islands as a Cultural Resource."

32. *Ber* is the Sea Island form of the word *Brer.*

33. Crum, *Gullah,* p. 55.

34. Quoted in ibid., p. 60.

35. This observation may in part answer a question posed by Richard Dorson, an avid researcher and collector of black folktales. Dorson observes that southern blacks drew a fair portion of their folktale material from the barnyards, fields, and woods which formed their environment. "Why they neglected such familiar denizens as the coon and the possum," he comments, "in favor of the rabbit and the fox, and preferred the buzzard over the owl, remain teasing questions" (*American Negro Folktales* [New York: Fawcett, 1967], p. 67). Perhaps the questions are not "teasing" at all. The animals of the tales are intensely interesting to the islanders because they have had to study these animals so closely to learn to hunt them. According to some of the island storytellers—people who are also known for their hunting skills—such animals as the buzzard are revered for their patience. They are often used as foils to much smarter animals like the monkey or the rabbit. On the other hand, the rabbit is renowned for his cunning and his illusionary and evasive skills. Though his teeth are sharp, he has no

protective coating like Ber Cooter. He cannot fly like Ber Buzzard or remain aloof on a high perch like the owl. His only defense is his wit, and his wit he puts to good use in the tales told about him on the Sea Islands. Knowing his habits well, perhaps the islanders find him more deserving of the titles "trister" and "sporty little animal" than any of the other animals they come in contact with.

36. The islanders' interactions with the natural environment go beyond the economic. The children become amateur oceanographers and learn to foretell the weather by the humidity and color of the sun at given times of the day, and the manner in which it sets in the evening. They learn to gauge time within minutes in a furrowed field by counting the number of rows that a shadow covers at certain times of the day, as well as by the distance of the sun as it moves from "day clean"—sunrise—to "out the light"—sunset. "Island time" is important because the inhabitants fish, crab, and shrimp only when the tide reaches certain levels coming in or going out. Water is a subject of much symbolism among the older islanders. Once one has partaken of the Sea Island water, one is thought to have a right to live on the islands. But as I was informed, in no uncertain terms, the water must be *offered* by an older, native-born member of high social esteem for that right to be legitimized.

37. On this point see, for example, Joyner, *Down by the Riverside,* pp. 61–63.

38. Winifred Owens (personal communication).

39. Mary Arnold Twining, "An Examination of African Retention in the Folk Culture of the South Carolina and Georgia Sea Islands" (Ph.D. diss., Indiana University, 1977), p. 175.

40. Ibid.; Owens (personal communication).

41. Greg Day, *South Carolina Low Country Coil Baskets* (Charleston, S.C.: Charleston Communication Center, n.d.).

42. Jackson, Slaughter, and Blake, "The Sea Islands as a Cultural Resource," p. 37.

43. William Demerson (Bamidele Ade Agbasebe), *The Role of Wife in The Black Extended Family: Perspectives from a Rural Community in the Southern United States,* New Research on Women and Sex Roles (Ann Arbor: University of Michigan Center for Continuing Education of Women, 1974), p. 135. Demerson is an anthropologist who has spent several years in the Sea Island area.

44. Ibid., p. 130.

45. Ibid., p. 135.

46. For further discussion see Joyner, *Down by the Riverside,* pp. 141–63, especially p. 144.

47. W. D. Weatherford, *The Negro from Africa to America* (1924; reprint, New York: Negro Universities Press, 1969), p. 44.

48. See John S. Mbiti, *African Religions and Philosophy* (New York: Doubleday and Co., Anchor Books, 1970), p. 209.

49. Quoted in Patricia Jones-Jackson, "The Status of Guallah: An Investigation of Convergent Processes" (Ph.D. diss., University of Michigan, 1978), p. 134. See also Appendix 3 herein.

50. Georgia Writers Project, *Drums and Shadows,* p. 236.

51. Crum, for example, does not acknowledge the influence of African languages

on the speech of the islands, but he does, without qualification, admit the African origin of the traditional burial customs (*Gullah,* p. 97).

52. Robert Hamill Nassau, *Fetichism in West Africa* (New York: Charles Scribner's Sons, 1904), p. 218.

53. Emory Campbell (personal communication), Penn School Center, Frogmore, S.C.

54. Quoted in Patricia Jones-Jackson, "The Oral Tradition of Prayer in Gullah," *Journal of Religious Thought* 39, no. 1 (Spring/Summer 1982): 22.

55. See Melville J. Herskovits, *The Myth of the Negro Past* (New York: Harper, 1941).

56. Jennett Robinson Murphy, *Southern Thought for Northern Thinkers* (New York, 1904), p. 23, quoted in Crum, *Gullah,* p. 144.

## Chapter 2

1. See Joel Chandler Harris, *Nights with Uncle Remus: Myths and Legends of the Old Plantation* (New York, 1883); Charles C. Jones, *Negro Myths from the Georgia Coast Told in the Vernacular* (Boston, Mass., 1888; reprint, Columbia, S.C.: State Co. 1925); Elsie Clews Parsons, *Folklore of the Sea Islands, South Carolina* (Cambridge, Mass.: American Folklore Society, 1923); and Ambrose Gonzales, *With Aesop along the Black Border* (Columbia, S.C.: The State Co., 1924).

2. See Charles Joyner, "Slave Folklife on the Waccamaw Neck" (Ph.D. diss., University of Pennsylvania, 1977); or Joyner, *Down by the Riverside,* pp. 172–195, especially pp. 190–91.

3. The *he* is for convenience; Sea Island storytellers can be women but are more usually men (see the next section of this chapter).

4. Lee Haring, "A Characteristic African Folktale Pattern," and Phillip Noss, "Description in Gbaya Literary Art," both in *African Folklore,* ed. Richard Dorson (Bloomington: Indiana University Press, 1972); and Patricia Jones-Jackson, "The Audience in Gullah and Igbo: A Comparison of Oral Traditions," *College Language Association Journal* 27, no. 2 (December 1983): 197–209.

5. DeCamp, "Toward a Generative Analysis," p. 369.

6. Dell Hymes, *Foundations in Sociolinguistics: An Ethnographic Approach* (Philadelphia: University of Pennsylvania, 1974), pp. 43–44.

7. Ray L. Birdwhistell, *Kinesics and Context: Essays on Body Motion Communication* (Philadelphia: University of Pennsylvania Press, 1970), pp. 80–81.

8. Alfred Hayes, "Paralinguistics and Kinesics: Pedagogical Perspectives," in *Approaches to Semiotics,* ed. Thomas Sebeok, Alfred S. Hayes, and Mary C. Bateson (London: Mouton Publishers, 1964), pp. 158–59.

9. Richard Dorson, *Negro Tales from Pine Bluff, Arkansas, and Calvin, Michigan* (Bloomington: Indiana University Press, 1958), p. 52.

10. "Description in Gbaya Literary Art," p. 74.

11. Finnegan, *Limba Stories,* p. 68.

12. Interview courtesy of WHMM TV and South Carolina ETV, from the documentary film *When Roots Die,* 1985.

## Chapter 3

1. The prayers are often presented in a chanting style difficult for non-Gullah speakers to understand. Thus I gratefully acknowledge the aid of Mrs. Ida Morris-Hamilton of Wadmalaw Island for helping with transcriptions and translations.

2. See Mbiti, *African Religions and Philosophy;* Harold Carter, *The Prayer Tradition of Black People* (Valley Forge, Pa.: Judson Press, 1976); William H. Pipes, *Say Amen Brother* (New York: William Federal Press, 1951); and Jones-Jackson, "Oral Tradition."

3. The prayers are normally accompanied by music. If no musical accompanist is available, the prayer giver and the congregation create their own musical accompaniment with handclaps, shuffles, and moans.

4. See Carter, *Prayer Tradition;* Pipes, *Say Amen Brother;* and Molefe Asante, *African and African-American Communication Continuities* (New York: Council of International Studies, State University of New York at Buffalo, 1975).

5. This prayer was delivered impromptu by Mr. James Brown, who is known for his ability to deliver stirring words with absolutely no prior preparation. I am grateful to him and Rev. Renty Pinckney for permitting me to record this prayer during church services. I am likewise grateful to Rev. Chester R. Jones for his comments on my analysis of the prayer. I owe special thanks to Rev. Alfred Owens of Greater Mt. Calvary Holy Church, Washington, D.C., for his invaluable assistance in providing references for the many biblical allusions in the prayer. All references are to the King James Version.

6. Ps. 51, David's cry for repentance and mercy, may have been a model for this passage.

7. Matt. 8:20; Luke 9:58.

8. Rom. 6:12, 8:11; 1 Cor. 15:53–54; John 15:1.

9. Matt. 4:3; 1 Thess. 3:5.

10. John 1:32.

11. Phil. 3:13.

12. Ps. 1:14.

13. John 12:2, 25:4.

14. 2 Cor. 7:5.

15. The speaker adapts his prayer to fit the occasion by including the purpose for which he is offering his prayer in strategic places. Many of the following passages are based on the Sermon on the Mount and the Beatitudes; the speaker brings them into his prayer as responses (e.g., "Want my spirit meek and mild").

16. The minister is often considered the assembler and leader of the community as well as of the church. Thus, like Moses, he is viewed as a deliverer of the people, one chosen by God to be the inheritor of the silver trumpet. See Num. 10:1–10.

17. This is a rural expression of the idea from Matt. 7:24–29 that whosoever builds his house on solid rock shall not be moved by the storms of life.

18. Jerusalem is not only the holy biblical city but, literally, the name of the AME church in which this prayer was delivered.

19. 1 Cor. 15:53–54.

20. "Ain't gonna study war no more" is a reference from an old Negro spiritual. The concept itself comes from several references to war in the Bible, such as Ps. 46:0, Isa. 2:4, and Mic. 4:3.

21. Rom. 14:10–12; 2 Cor. 5:10; Matt. 16–27.

22. Job 3:17.

23. I am again indebted to Mrs. Ida Morris-Hamilton, who assisted in transcribing this sermon from a recording made during the church service.

24. For further discussion of the call-and-response technique see Grace Sims Holt, "Stylin' outta the Black Pulpit," in *Rappin' and Stylin' Out,* ed. Thomas Kochman (Urbana: University of Illinois Press, 1972), pp. 189–204.

25. The Gullah and African tales given in this chapter are classified according to the scheme set out by Antti Aarne and Stith Thompson in *The Types of the Folktale* (Helsinki: *Suomalainen Tiedeakatenia,* 1961). Motifs and the names and numbers assigned to tale types are from Stith Thompson, *Motif-Index of Folk Literature,* 6 vols. (Bloomington: Indiana University Press, 1955–58).

In the search for systematic methods of presenting such paralinguistic features as voice quality and nonverbal expressive phenomena, Ray L. Birdwhistell proposed a system of notation for describing certain sound phenomena, for example, an arrow pointing upward or downward to indicate various pitch ranges. He likewise developed an elaborate notational system for analyzing body motions and gestures, a system that distinguished hip, leg, ankle, shoulder, wrist, arm, and other movements (see Birdwhistell, *Kinesics and Context*). Some of these notations are quite complex, and they are not yet widely used. Here, because the language of the narratives is complex in itself for most English-speaking readers, I decided to eliminate reading handicaps by minimizing foreign symbols that would tend to interrupt the natural flow of the tales.

26. For example, Richard Dorson has a variant of this tale in *American Negro Folktales,* p. 114.

27. This observation was brought to my attention by Charles Joyner, who is a native of the South Carolina coastal area.

28. See Harris, *Nights with Uncle Remus;* Parsons, *Folklore of the Sea Islands;* Finnegan, *Limba Stories;* Florence M. Cronise and Henry Ward, *Cunnie Rabbit, Mr. Spider and the Other Beef* (Chicago: Afro-Am Press, 1969); and Dorson, *African Folklore.*

29. The precautionary measures taken here do not assure that the Igbo tales collected were not influenced by other cultures. No culture can be totally without outside influence; I tried only to decrease the likelihood of obtaining tales with non-African origins. Accordingly, I collected the tales from children and adults only in their native tongue. Although English is a second language in Nigeria, those in remote areas have little reason to use it. I also did not ask to hear any particular type of tale, nor put any restrictions on the length or number of tales told by any one person. I asked simply to hear some of their stories.

30. I am indebted to the renowned Igbo writer Obi Egbuna for his observations concerning African folktales and their implications in Igbo society. Any misrepresentations that might remain are, of course, my own.

31. See Cronise and Ward, *Cunnie Rabbit.*

32. See Finnegan, *Limba Stories;* and Cronise and Ward, *Cunnie Rabbit.*

33. See Harris, *Nights with Uncle Remus;* and Martha Warren Beckwith, *Jamaica Anansi Stories* (New York: American Folklore Society, 1924).

34. See Dorson, *African Folklore;* and Parsons, *Folklore of the Sea Islands.*


## Chapter 4

1. On *Gullah* see Wood, *Black Majority,* p. 335. For *Geechee* see Turner, *Africanisms in the Gullah Dialect,* p. 194. As many as 70 percent of the slaves brought to the Sea Islands may have come from Angola. As far back as 1822, the Charleston City Council regarded the word *Gullah* as a corruption of *Angola.* John G. Williams wrote in the *Charleston Sunday News,* 10 February 1895: "Gullah is very probably a corruption of Angola, shortened to Gola, a country of West Africa, and part of Lower Guinea, from which a great many negroes were brought to this country in the days of the slave trade. I remember hearing the old plantation negroes before the war speak of one as a 'Gullah nigger' and another as a 'Guinea nigger.' " When members of the Georgia Writers Project of 1940 asked an elderly man if he could remember any of the people brought over from Africa, he replied: " 'Yas, I know heaps ub um. Deah wuz "Golla" John Wiley, "Golla" Jim Bayfield—he wuz bought by Mahse Charles Lamar, and he sole im to Mr. McMullen. Den deah wuz "Golla" Jack, "Golla" Tom, "Golla" Silvie, "Golla" Charles Carr. . . . All duh people wut come frum Africa aw obushseas wuz call "Golla," and dey talk wuz call "Golla" talk' " (*Drums and Shadows,* p. 66).

2. Turner, *Africanisms in the Gullah Dialect.*

3. Water is symbolic of life, happiness, and goodwill on the Sea Islands, and water from certain areas on the islands is felt to have curative properties. Thus Francis's reply is not without some merit.

4. For early studies on Gullah see George Phillip Krapp, "The English of the American Negro," *American Mercury* 2 (June 1924): 190–95; Reed Smith, *Gullah,* Bulletin of the '    iversity of South Carolina, no. 190 (Columbia: *University of South Carolina Pr      ,*26); and H. L. Mencken, *The American Language: Supplement II* (New York: Knopf, 1942).

5. Ambrose E. Gonzales, *The Black Border* (Columbia, S.C.: The State Co., 1922), p. 10.

6. Turner, *Africanisms in the Gullah Dialect,* p. 296.

7. To take one interesting example of nonstandard speech, Ian Hancock has recently informed me that an African-Seminole variety of English is spoken in Oklahoma and Texas. This mixture is unsurprising: Africans and Indians have coexisted since the beginning of foreign migrations into America.

8. See Irma Cunningham, "A Syntactic Analysis of Sea Island Creole (Gullah)." (Ph.D. diss., University of Michigan; 1970); Nichols, *Linguistic Change in Gullah;* Joyner, "Slave Folklife," or *Down by the Riverside,* pp. 196–224; and Jones-Jackson, "The Status of Gullah."

9. See DeCamp, "Toward a Generative Analysis."

10. The African derivations of these words are from Turner, *Africanisms in the Gullah Dialect*.

11. For a critical appraisal of Turner's methodology see P. E. H. Hair, "Sierra Leone Items in the Gullah Dialect of American English," *African Language Review* 4 (1965): 79–84.

12. DeCamp, Foreword to Turner, *Africanisms in the Gullah Dialect*, pp. vii–viii.

13. For a detailed discussion of the processes involved in language contact see Talmy Givón, "Prolegomena to Any Creology" (Department of Linguistics, University of California, Los Angeles, Mimeo, 1973).

14. According to Wolfram (personal communication), the "matrix of cruciality" refers to linguistic features that are important to control in situations where one would be expected to use a form of standard English.

15. For a fuller syntactical analysis of Gullah than follows here, see Cunningham, "Syntactic Analysis." See Jones-Jackson, "The Status of Gullah," for a full representation of creole features in context.

16. See Turner, *Africanisms in the Gullah Dialect*, p. 225.

17. See Dietrich Westerman and M. A. Bryan, *The Languages of West Africa* (London: Oxford University Press, 1952).

18. Turner, *Africanisms in the Gullah Dialect*, p. 211.

19. See Nichols, "Linguistic Change in Gullah," for a detailed discussion and historical analysis of the complementizer *for*.

20. J. L. Dillard, *Black English* (New York: Random House, 1972).


## Appendix 1

1. Jackson, Slaughter, and Blake, "The Sea Islands as a Cultural Resource."


## Appendix 3

1. For a full discussion of the phonemes in Gullah, see Jones-Jackson, "The Status of Gullah," and Turner, *Africanisms in the Gullah Dialect*.


## Appendix 4

1. All quotations in this appendix are from the film documentary *When Roots Die*, produced by me in conjunction with WHMM TV at Howard University and the South Carolina ETV network. I owe special thanks to Charles Sessoms, who helped to write and who directed the film. Likewise, I am indebted to Henry Cauthens, director of the South Carolina ETV network, for providing a crew (Patrice Abrams, Jimmy Dinkins, and Joe Bowie) to undertake the filming in South Carolina; and to Edward Hawthorne, dean of the Graduate School of Arts and Sciences, and Arnold Wallace, general manager of WHMM TV, Howard University, for providing the funds.

2. Robert Browne, founder of the National Emergency Land Fund and research scholar for the Black Economic Research Center (personal communication).

# Selected Bibliography

Aarne, Antti, and Stith Thompson. *The Types of the Folktale*. Helsinki: Suomalainen Tiedeakatenia, 1961.

Abrahams, Roger D. *Deep Down in the Jungle*. Chicago: Aldine Publishing Co., 1963.

Asante, Molefe. *African and African-American Communication Continuities*. New York: Council on International Studies, State University of New York at Buffalo, 1975.

_____. *Rhetoric of Black Revolution*. Boston: Allyn and Bacon, 1970.

Baird, Keith E. "Guy B. Johnson Revisited: Another Look at Gullah." *Journal of Black Studies* 10, no. 4 (June 1980): 425–36.

Bancroft, Frederic. *Slave Trading in the Old South*. Baltimore: J. J. Furst Co., 1931.

Beckwith, Martha Warren. *Jamaica Anansi Stories*. New York: American Folklore Society, 1924.

Bennett, John. "Gullah: A Negro Patois." *South Atlantic Quarterly* 7, no. 4 (October 1908): 332–47.

Berkeley-Charleston-Dorchester (BCD) Council of Governments. *Regional Housing Market Analysis*. 1979.

_____. *Report on Economically Less Developed Areas in the Berkeley Charleston Dorchester Region*. 1980.

Bickerton, Derek. *Dynamic of a Creole System*. Cambridge: Cambridge University Press, 1975.

_____. "On the Nature of a Creole Continuum." *Language* 39 (1973): 640–69.

_____. *Roots of Language*. Ann Arbor, Mich.: Karoma Press, 1981.

Birdwhistell, Ray L. *Kinesics and Context: Essays on Body Motion Communication*. Philadelphia: University of Pennsylvania Press, 1970.

Brunvand, Jan Harold. *The Study of American Folklore*. New York: W. W. Norton and Co., 1968.

Carter, Harold. *The Prayer Tradition of Black People*. Valley Forge, Pa.: Judson Press, 1976.

Christophersen, Merrill G. *Biography of an Island*. Fennimore, Wis.: Westburg Assoc., 1976.

Clark, Verney R. "Preserved Africanisms in the New World." *Afro-World Religious Research Series* 3, no. 1 (June 1974): 1–62.

Cronise, Florence M., and Henry Ward. *Cunnie Rabbit, Mr. Spider and the Other Beef.* Chicago: Afro-Am Press, 1969.

Crum, Mason. *Gullah: Negro Life in the Carolina Sea Islands.* Durham, N.C.: Duke University Press, 1940.

Cunningham, Irma. "A Syntactic Analysis of Sea Island Creole (Gullah)." Ph.D. diss., University of Michigan, 1970.

Curtin, Philip D. *The Atlantic Slave Trade.* Madison: University of Wisconsin Press, 1969.

Davis, Gerald L. "Afro-American Coil Basketry in Charleston County, South Carolina: Affective Characteristics of an Artistic Craft in a Social Context." In *American Folklife,* edited by Don Yoder. Austin: University of Texas Press, 1976.

Day, Greg. *South Carolina Low Country Coil Baskets.* Charleston, S. C.: Charleston Communication Center, n.d.

DeCamp, David. "Toward a Generative Analysis of a Post-Creole Speech Continuum." *Pidginization and Creolization of Languages,* edited by Dell Hymes. Cambridge: Cambridge University Press, 1971.

DeCamp, David, and Ian F. Hancock, eds. *Pidgins and Creoles: Current Trends and Prospects.* Washington, D.C.: Georgetown University Press, 1974.

Demerson, William (Bamidele Ade Agbasebe). *The Role of Wife in the Black Extended Family: Perspectives from a Rural Community in the Southern United States.* New Research on Women and Sex Roles. Ann Arbor: University of Michigan Center for Continuing Education of Women, 1974.

Dillard, J. L. *Black English.* New York: Random House, 1972.

Donnan, Elizabeth. *Documents Illustrative of the History of the Slave Trade to America.* Vol. 4. Washington, D.C.: Carnegie Institution of Washington, 1930.

Dorian, Nancy C. "The Fate of Morphological Complexity in Language Death: Evidence from East Sutherland Gaelic." *Language* 54 (1978): 590–609.

Dorson, Richard. *American Negro Folktales.* New York: Fawcett, 1967.

————. *Folktales Told Around the World.* Chicago: University of Chicago Press, 1975.

————. *Negro Tales from Pine Bluff, Arkansas, and Calvin, Michigan.* Bloomington: Indiana University Press, 1958.

————. "Oral Styles of American Folk Narrators." In *Style in Language,* edited by Thomas Sebeok. New York: Technology Press and John Wiley and Sons, 1960.

————, ed. *African Folklore.* Bloomington: Indiana University Press, 1972.

Fasold, Ralph. *Tense Marking in Black English: A Linguistic and Social Analysis.* Arlington, Va.: Center for Applied Linguistics, 1972.

Finnegan, Ruth. *Limba Stories and Storytelling.* Oxford: Oxford University Press, 1969.

Fisher, John H., and Diane Barnstein. *A Forme of Speech in Chaunge: Readings in the History of the English Language.* Englewood Cliffs, N.J.: Prentice-Hall, 1974.

Givón, Talmy. "Prolegomena to Any Creology." Department of Linguistics, University of California, Los Angeles. Mimeo, 1973.

Goldstein, Kenneth. *A Guide for Field Workers in Folklore.* Hatboro, N.C.: Folklore Assoc., 1964.

Gonzales, Ambrose. *The Black Border.* Columbia, S.C.: The State Co., 1922.

_____. *With Aesop along the Black Border*. Columbia, S.C.: The State Co., 1924.

Hair, P. E. H. "Sierra Leone Items in the Gullah Dialect of American English." *African Language Review* 4 (1965): 79–84.

Hancock, Ian. "Gullah and Barbadian: Origins and Relationships." *American Speech* 55, no. 1 :(1980) 17–35.

_____. *The Texas Seminoles and Their Language*. African and Afro-American Studies and Research Center Monograph Series 2, no. 1. Austin: University of Texas, 1980.

Haring, Lee. "A Characteristic African Folktale Pattern." In *African Folklore*, edited by Richard Dorson. Bloomington: Indiana University Press, 1972.

Harris, Joel Chandler. *Nights with Uncle Remus: Myths and Legends of the Old Plantation*. New York, 1883.

Hayes, Alfred. "Paralinguistics and Kinesics: Pedagogical Perspectives." In *Approaches to Semiotics*, edited by Thomas Sebeok, Alfred S. Hayes, and Mary C. Bateson. London: Mouton Publishers, 1964.

Holt, Grace Sims. "Stylin' outta the Black Pulpit." In *Rappin' and Stylin' Out*, edited by Thomas Kochman. Urbana: University of Illinois Press, 1972.

Hymes, Dell. "The Contribution of Folklore to Sociolinguistic Research." In *Toward New Perspectives in Folklore*, edited by Americo Paredes and Richard Bauman. Austin: University of Texas Press, 1975.

_____. *Foundations in Sociolinguistics: An Ethnographic Approach*. Philadelphia: University of Pennsylvania Press, 1974.

Jackson, Juanita, Sabra Slaughter, and J. Herman Blake. "The Sea Islands as a Cultural Resource." *Black Scholar*, March 1974, pp. 32–39.

Johnson, Guion. *A Social History of the Sea Islands with Special References to St. Helena Island, South Carolina*. Chapel Hill: University of North Carolina Press, 1930.

Johnson, Guy B. *Folk Culture of St. Helena Island*. Chapel Hill: University of North Carolina Press, 1930.

_____. "The Gullah Dialect Revisited: A Note on Linguistic Acculturation." *Journal of Black Studies* 10, no. 4 (June 1980): 417–24.

Johnson, Bishop Joseph A. *The Soul of the Black Preacher*. New York: Pilgram Press, 1961.

Jones, Charles C. *Negro Myths from the Georgia Coast Told in the Vernacular*. Boston: Riverside Press, 1888. Reprint. Columbia, S.C.: State Co., 1925.

Jones, Eldred. "Krio: An English-Based Language of Sierra Leone." In *The English Language in West Africa*, edited by J. Spencer. London: Longman, 1971.

Jones-Jackson, Patricia. "The Audience in Gullah and Igbo: A Comparison of Oral Traditions." *College Language Association Journal* 27, no. 2 (December 1983): 197–209.

_____. "Gullah: On the Question of Afro-American Language." *Anthropological Linguistics* 20, no. 9 (December 1978): 422–27.

_____. "On Decreolization and Language Death in Gullah." *Language in Society* 13 (Fall 1984): 351–62.

_____. "The Oral Tradition of Prayer in Gullah." *Journal of Religious Thought* 39, no. 1 (Spring/Summer 1982): 21–33.

————. "The Status of Gullah: An Investigation of Convergent Processes." Ph.D. Diss., University of Michigan, 1978.

Joyner, Charles. *Down by the Riverside: A South Carolina Slave Community.* Urbana: University of Illinois Press, 1984.

————. "Slave Folklife on the Waccamaw Neck." Ph.D. diss., University of Pennsylvania, 1977.

Krapp, George Phillip. "The English of the American Negro." *American Mercury* 2 (June 1924): 190–95.

Labarre, Weston. "Paralinguistics, Kinesics, and Cultural Anthropology." In *Approaches to Semiotics,* edited by Thomas Sebeok, Alfred S. Hayes, and Mary C. Bateson. London: Mouton Publishers, 1964.

Labov, William. *Language in the Inner-City.* Philadelphia: University of Pennsylvania Press, 1972.

Lawton, David. "Suprasegmental Phonics in Jamaican Creole." Ph.D. diss., Michigan State University, 1963.

LeConte, Joseph. *Autobiography.* New York, 1903.

Martinet, André. *Éléments de linguistique générale.* Paris: Librairie Armand Colin, 1960.

Mbiti, John S. *African Religions and Philosophy.* New York: Doubleday and Co., Anchor Books, 1970.

Mencken, H. L. *The American Language: Supplement II.* New York: Knopf, 1948.

Mitchell, Faith. *Hoodoo Medicine: Sea Island Herbal Remedies.* Berkeley, Calif.: Reed, Cannon and Johnson Co., 1978.

Mitchell, Henry. *Black Preaching.* Philadelphia: J. B. Lippincott Co., 1970.

Montgomery, Michael, ed. *Language Variety in the South: Perspectives in Black and White.* Tuscaloosa: University of Alabama Press, 1986.

Moore, Janice G. "Africanisms among Blacks of the Sea Islands." *Journal of Black Studies* 10, no. 4 (June 1980): 467–80.

Mufwene, Salikoko. "Number Delimitation in Gullah." *American Speech.* Forthcoming.

Nassau, Robert Hamill. *Fetichism in West Africa.* New York: Charles Scribner's Sons, 1904.

Nichols, Patricia. "Linguistic Change in Gullah: Sex, Age, and Mobility." Ph.D. diss., Stanford University, 1976.

Noss, Phillip. "Description in Gbaya Literary Art." In *African Folklore,* edited by Richard Dorson. Bloomington: Indiana University Press, 1972.

Osgood, Charles E. "Universals in Psycholinguistics." In *Universals of Language,* edited by Joseph H. Greenberg. Cambridge, Mass.: MIT Press, 1963.

Paredes, Americo, and Richard Bauman, eds. *Toward New Perspectives in Folklore.* Austin: University of Texas Press, 1975.

Parsons, Elsie Clews. *Folklore of the Sea Islands, South Carolina.* Cambridge, Mass.: American Folklore Society, 1923.

Pipes, William H. *Say Amen Brother.* New York: William Federal Press, 1951.

Rickford, John. "The Insights of the Mesolect." In *Pidgins and Creoles: Current Trends and Prospects,* edited by David DeCamp and Ian F. Hancock. Washington, D.C.: Georgetown University Press, 1974.

Saunders, William C. "Sea Islands: Then and Now." *Journal of Black Studies* 10, no. 4 (June 1980): 481–92.

Sebeok, Thomas A., ed. *Style in Language.* New York: Technology Press and John Wiley and Sons, 1960.

Sebeok, Thomas, Alfred S. Hayes, and Mary C. Bateson, eds. *Approaches to Semiotics.* London: Mouton Publishers, 1964.

Smith, Reed. *Gullah.* Bulletin of the University of South Carolina, no. 190. Columbia: University of South Carolina Press, 1926.

Tedlock, Dennis. "On the Translation of Style in Oral Narrative." In *Toward New Perspectives in Folklore,* edited by Americo Paredes and Richard Bauman. Austin: University of Texas Press, 1975.

Thomas, June Manning. "The Impact of Corporate Tourism on Gullah Blacks: Notes on Issues of Employment." *Phylon* 41, no. 1 (Spring 1980): 1–11.

Thompson, Stith. *Motif-Index of Folk Literature.* 6 vols. Bloomington: Indiana University Press, 1955–58.

Traugott, Elizabeth. "Some Thoughts on Natural Syntactic Processes." In *New Ways of Analyzing Variation in English,* edited by C. J. N. Bailey and Roger Shuy. Washington: Georgetown University Press, 1973.

Turner, Lorenzo D. *Africanisms in the Gullah Dialect.* Chicago: University of Chicago Press, 1949.

Twining, Mary Arnold. "An Examination of African Retention in the Folk Culture of the South Carolina and Georgia Sea Islands." Ph.D., diss., Indiana University, 1977.

Waccamaw Regional Planning and Development Council. *Waccamaw Regional Housing Element,* 1977.

Weatherford, W. D. *The Negro From Africa to America.* 1924. Reprint. New York: Negro Universities Press, 1969.

Westerman, Dietrich, and M. A. Bryan. *The Languages of West Africa.* London: Oxford University Press, 1952.

Wikramanayake, Marina. *A World in Shadow: The Free Black in Antebellum South Carolina.* Columbia: University of South Carolina Press, 1973.

Williams, John G. 1895. "Is Gullah A Corruption of Angola?" *Charleston, S.C., Sunday News,* 10 February 1895.

Wolfram, Walt. *A Sociolinguistic Description of Detroit Negro Speech.* Washington, D.C.: Center for Applied Linguistics, 1969.

Wood, Peter H. *Black Majority: Negroes in Colonial South Carolina from 1690 through the Stone Rebellion.* New York: Alfred A. Knopf, 1974.

# Index